Boys and Literacy

Boys and Literacy

Practical Strategies for Librarians, Teachers, and Parents

Elizabeth Knowles and Martha Smith

LIBRARIES
U N L I M I T E D
A Member of the Greenwood Publishing Group

Westport, Connecticut • London

40.00

Library of Congress Cataloging-in-Publication Data

Knowles, Elizabeth, 19460
  Boys and literacy : practical strategies for librarians, teachers, and parents / Elizabeth
Knowles and Martha Smith.
   p. cm.
  Includes bibliographical references and index
  ISBN 1-59158-212-1 (pbk. : alk. paper)
  1. Boys—Books and reading—United States. 2. Children's literature,
American—Bibliography. 3. Young adult literature, American—Bibliography. 4.
Reading—Sex differences. I. Smith, Martha, 1946- II. Title.
Z1039.B67K66 2005
028.5'5—dc22 2004063830

British Library Cataloguing in Publication Data is available.

Library of Congress Catalog Card Number: 2004063830
ISBN: 1-59158-212-1

First published in 2005

Libraries Unlimited, 88 Post Road West, Westport, CT 06881
A Member of the Greenwood Publishing Group, Inc.
www.lu.com

Printed in the United States of America

The paper used in this book complies with the
Permanent Paper Standard issued by the National
Information Standards Organization (Z39.48-1984).

10 9 8 7 6 5 4 3 2

Contents

Introduction

A surprising amount of research has appeared in the last five years about boys and what is happening to them academically at school, especially in the area of literacy. The research is continuing into the university and graduate school years and even drawing from current brain research.

The situation appears to be serious, so much so that resources advising teachers and parents what to do differently with boys and learning are appearing frequently. It will be necessary for all involved to read the research, recognize the issues, and then make the commitment to create a difference for the sake of boys.

We have included a section that provides strategies for change for teachers and parents and a whole school reading plan that suggests a paradigm shift in the approach to reading, with special focus on the needs of boys.

There are 11 genre chapters: humor, adventure, information/nonfiction, fantasy/science fiction, horror/mystery, sports, war, biography, history, graphic novels, and realistic fiction. Each chapter contains generic discussion questions, annotated titles, and a bibliography sorted by topic, nonfiction, and picture books where appropriate. There is also an annotated professional journal article.

Since authors often share interesting anecdotes about their school years and their early feelings about reading and writing, appendix A provides author information including contact information to encourage teachers, librarians, and parents to connect with these authors and learn more about them. Often authors will respond to letters and e-mails, and certainly publicists will send photos, bookmarks, biographical information, etc. With the author information we have included extensive booklists, since we have found that boys like to read all the titles a favorite author has published. We found the online subscription database at http://www.authors4teens.com to be a valuable resource and would like to thank Greenwood Publishing for allowing us to utilize the information for our authors' section. We have also found Bernard Drew's *100 More Popular Young Adult Authors* (Libraries Unlimited, 2002) and Sharron McElmeel's *Children's Authors and Illustrators Too Good to Miss* (Libraries Unlimited, 2004) to be excellent resources for information on authors that can be easily shared with students. Since we are encouraging students to contact these authors, we have included only living authors.

Since we also strongly believe in the use of magazines for piquing boys' reading interests, appendix B lists magazines boys will enjoy. Each listing gives a description, appropriate age levels, and complete subscription information. We would also like to recommend another wonderful resource from Libraries Unlimited, the *Children's Magazine Guide: A Subject Index to Children's Magazines and Web Sites,* published at the end of each month. See http://www.childrensmag.com for subscription pricing and information. The information on magazines used in this book is used with permission from Kristina Sheppard, the editor of the *Children's Magazine Guide.*

We also recognize the up-and-coming graphic novel area. These novels are a wonderful way to entice boys, as they feature superheroes, quests, monsters, and strange adventures. We are finding that more and more publishers are including a "graphic novel" format in their publishing list and that DC Comics,

Dark Horse, and others are gaining new momentum in this area as it grows in its appeal to teens and preteens. There is a whole new list of authors, illustrators, and terminology, including "manga," the Japanese word for comic, and the whole concept of reading a novel from right to left or back to front! We found an excellent resource specifically for librarians and teachers: Allyson A. W. Lyga, with Barry Lyga, *Graphic Novels in Your Media Center: A Definitive Guide* (Libraries Unlimited, 2004). It includes summaries, background information, and ideas for getting teachers interested and for selecting the best titles. We are including a thorough annotation of this resource in the chapter on graphic novels.

It is very important to make boys feel comfortable about their reading and to give them a voice to respond to it. We recommend book discussion groups and literature circles where boys can write, draw, and talk about the things they read in a comfortable, nonthreatening atmosphere. We have included several excellent resources for information about literature circles and book discussion groups in our Resources section. Building a connection with books is extremely worthwhile, and these types of activities allow for thoughtful, casual, and empowering responses to reading.

We used *Books in Print* (BIP) at http://www.booksinprint.com and John Gillespie and Catherine Barr's *Best Books for Middle School and Junior High Readers* (Libraries Unlimited, 2004) for grade level placement and genre classification. We realize that the grade level placement is arbitrary, and it is used to suggest the level for the books in the hopes that all readers will find suitable reading material.

The following abbreviations are used to indicate reading/interest level:

Adult	written for adults but accessible to younger readers
Gr.	grade(s)
Juv	juvenile
YA Mature	mature reader
YA	young adult

What Does
the Research Say?

Conlin (2003) wrote a cover story for *Business Week* with a rather startling title, "The New Gender Gap: From Kindergarten to Grad School, Boys Are Becoming the Second Sex." The article offers a summary of the recent trends seen across the nation and in most of the industrialized world at high schools and colleges. Girls are still doing better in reading, and now they are catching up in math and science. They are also participating more in clubs and activities—outnumbering boys in student government, the arts, yearbook and newspaper, academic clubs, and even sports teams. On the other hand, boys are far more likely to be found in special education classes and diagnosed with learning disabilities, emotional problems, and behavior problems. It is predicted that within this decade more undergraduate and graduate degrees will be awarded to women than men.

The article continues with some straight talk about education: Most elementary teachers are females who were educated 20 years ago, when gender was just a social function. The sit-still-and-listen mentality still reigns in many of the nation's classrooms. As a result more boys are diagnosed with ADHD and given Ritalin and other similar drugs in order for them to function in the classroom.

Mulrine (2001) published an article in *U.S. News & World Report*, "Are Boys the Weaker Sex?" in which she stated that boys' brains don't work quickly—they need time to ponder. She suggests that because boys' brains develop more slowly than girls' brains, it might be wise to let boys begin kindergarten a year older than girls. Mulrine also states that young boys are emotional and expressive, but it seems that parents, teachers, and peers change that by the time boys are school-aged, because the unwritten standard for boys is to hide emotions and expressiveness.

Noted children's author Jon Scieszka began a literacy initiative to call attention to the fact that boys and men are not reading. His Web site, http://www.guysread.com, offers lots of information about what is happening to boys in school and in the world in general. He challenges men to step up and become role models for boys by reading, for themselves and their sons and any other boys they come in contact with. The site has Scieszka's personal favorites and titles sent in and voted upon by boys. The lists are intended to be taken seriously by those who come in contact with boys.

Galley (2002), in an article in *Education Week*, commented on the National Assessment of Educational Progress (NAEP) scores in reading and writing, which put girls clearly ahead of boys in 4th, 8th, and 12th grades. She also pointed out that boys are better able to have close friendships and discuss their emotions at a young age than they are later in life, when the "big boys don't cry attitude" prevails. Galley also states that same-sex classes in middle school seem to be very beneficial for boys.

In a publication for middle school faculty and administration, *Voices from the Middle*, Jeff Wilhelm (2001) relates that boys like to read short passages and that they prefer books with lots of visual support, humor, a different perspective, and interesting facts. Classroom libraries, librarians, summer reading, and required course reading lists do not reflect the kinds of books that boys enjoy most.

Connell and Gunzelmann (2004), in *Scholastic Instructor*, describe boys as elementary outsiders because school curricula, classroom rules and organization, and expectations are beyond what most boys can accomplish. Sitting still, coloring in the lines, working together, being quiet, reading, writing, and speaking are all more difficult for most boys than for most girls. The authors share the damaging statistics about what is happening to boys inside and outside of school. They also offer some suggestions as to what parents and teachers can do to assist boys.

Too many boys do not have any positive role models for reading, is the message shared by Booth (2002) in *Even Hockey Players Read: Boys, Literacy, and Learning*. Booth states that reading is seen as something that females do and that there are too many distractions for boys. Boys would rather watch television, play computer games, or do something active. Since boys often have a difficult time learning to read, it is understandable that they do not see the pleasure in it, and since boys are usually very active, sitting quietly for a length of time to read a book is not very high on their list of favorite things to do.

Booth provides a long list of issues and problems regarding boys and literacy, including that boys have much less interest in leisure reading than girls, boys are two to five times more likely to have a reading disability than girls, boys rank lower in their class and earn fewer academic honors than girls, boys prefer active responses (dramatizing, demonstrating, etc.) to reading rather than discussion groups, boys who read are often teased by other boys, and boys are discouraged from responding emotionally to fiction by adults and other boys.

Pollack and Cushman (2001) write about the "Boy Code" in *Real Boys Workbook: The Definitive Guide to Understanding and Interacting with Boys of All Ages*. The code is unfortunately very prevalent in some cultures and families today. It is unwritten but clear that boys should be independent, separate from females as quickly as possible, never show feelings except anger, stay on top and in the limelight, bully and tease, not give in or listen, and not show fear of violence or tell on a boy who does something bad. This code indirectly impacts boys' attitudes in school and adds to the problems that they have.

Smith and Wilhelm (2002) in "Reading Don't Fix No Chevys: Literacy in the Lives of Young Men," share more information about the trouble boys are having with literacy. They state that boys take longer to learn to read and therefore read less than girls do, and they value reading less than girls. Nearly 50 percent of boys call themselves nonreaders by high school.

Newkirk (2002) makes some very interesting observations about literacy. Students today seem to prefer studying with friends, in front of the TV, or with music blaring rather than the silence and isolation of independent reading. He states that books are "instruments of immobilization"—the reader must be seated and quiet. Readers who enjoy reading and do it frequently do not consider sitting for long periods of time, absorbed in a story, to be difficult at all. An outsider or nonreader sees that as torture and unusual punishment—especially if the act of reading is difficult and the story is not easily understood.

Moir and Jessel (1992) state that one learns to read by hearing reading and by listening to readers. Boys are better at seeing than hearing, and that is the issue that makes it difficult for boys to learn to read. As long as education is the teacher talking and the student listening, then it is better set up for girls, who find it easier to listen than boys. The young male brain is into exploring, trying everything, and action, but the school wants him to sit quietly and listen.

Sullivan (2003) in *Connecting Boys with Books: What Librarians Can Do*, tells about the issues from a librarian's point of view. He says that boys rarely see a male children's librarian; there are simply no role models there. He also talks about the importance of after-school programs in public and school libraries because that is the time when many boys get into trouble—hanging out with their peers. He advises librarians to actively develop programs that will attract boys and encourage them to become regulars at the library.

Probably the best all-around guide for teachers and parents is Michael Gurian's (2001) *Boys and Girls Learn Differently: A Guide for Teachers and Parents*. Gurian covers the entire issue, from brain development and learning styles through what can be done about the problem. He states that girls take in more sensory data and are better with verbal communication than boys. He also states that chemically speaking, boys' brains secrete less serotonin than girls, which results in impulsivity and fidgeting. Boys tend to be deductive and abstract in their reasoning and more easily bored than girls. Cooperative and group learning is easier for girls—boys still adhere to pecking order and social strata and sometimes find it difficult to work together. Boys tend to be louder and more aggressive and more prone to attention-getting behaviors in the classroom, and therefore they often take up more of the teacher's time. Gurian also does an excellent job of providing solutions and strategies for teachers and parents in this book.

The following graphs and charts are included in their entirety from the U.S. Department of Education, Institute for Education Sciences, National Center for Education Statistics, *The Nation's Report Card: Writing Highlights 2002* (NCES 2003-531, by National Center for Education Statistics. Washington, D.C.: National Center for Education Statistics, 2003). Reprinted with permission. The information is much more meaningful when presented verbatim. Figures 1 through 4 show the gender comparison for two national testing years in the areas of reading and writing.

Figure 1. Average reading scale scores, by gender, grades 4 and 8: 1992–2003.

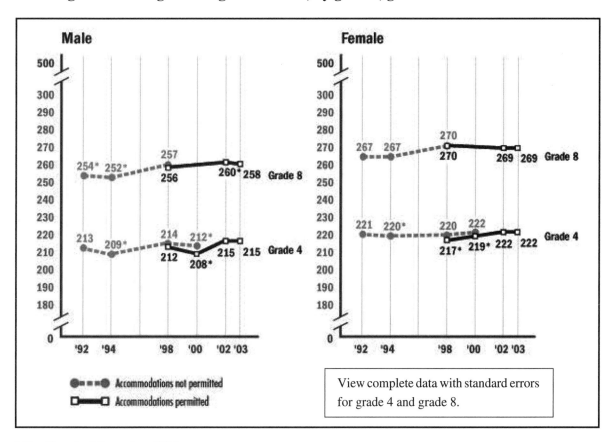

* Significantly different from 2003.

Note: Data were not collected at grade 8 in 2000. In addition to allowing for accommodations, the accommodations-permitted results at grade 4 (1998–2003) differ slightly from previous years' results, and from previously reported results for 1998 and 2000, due to changes in sample weighting procedures.

Significance tests were performed using unrounded numbers. NAEP sample sizes have increased since 2002 compared to previous years, resulting in smaller detectable differences than in previous assessments.

Source: U.S. Department of Education, Institute of Education Sciences, National Center for Education Statistics, *National Assessment of Educational Progress (NAEP)*, 1992, 1994, 1998, 2000, 2002, and 2003 Reading Assessments.

Major Findings

- There were no significant differences detected between the 2002 and 2003 average scores of male or female fourth-graders, nor between their 1992 and 2003 scores.

- The average reading score for male eighth-graders declined two points between 2002 and 2003, but the average score in 2003 was higher than in 1992.

- The average score for female eighth-graders in 2003 was not found to differ significantly from the scores in any of the previous assessment years.

- Female students scored higher on average than male students at both grades 4 and 8.

Figure 2. Gaps in average reading scale scores, by gender, grades 4 and 8: 1992–2003.

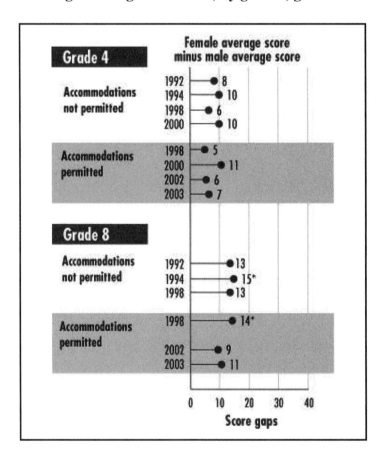

Major Findings

- In 2003, female students scored higher on average than male students by 7 points at grade 4, and by 11 points at grade 8.

- Between 2002 and 2003, there was no significant change detected in the score gaps between male students and female students.

- The fourth- and eighth-grade score gaps observed in 2003 were not found to be significantly different from those in 1992.

Figure 3. Average writing scale scores, by gender, grades 4, 8, and 12: 1998 and 2002.

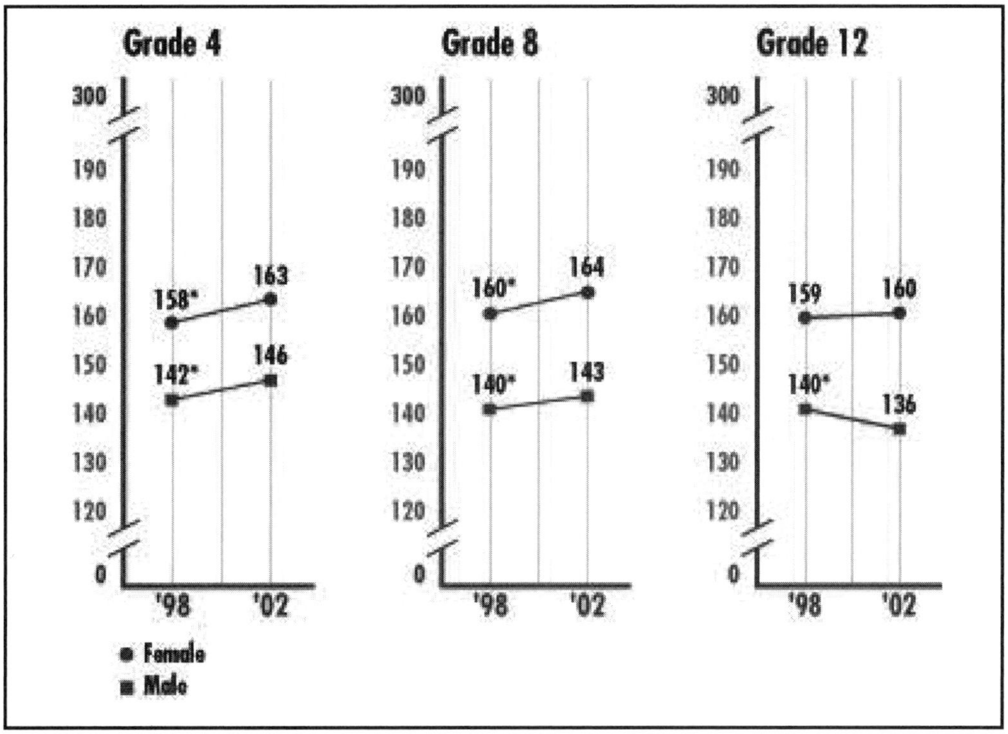

* Significantly different from 2002.

Source: U.S. Department of Education, Institute of Education Sciences, National Center for Education Statistics, *National Assessment of Educational Progress (NAEP),* 1998 and 2002 Writing Assessments.

Major Findings

• The average scores of male and female fourth-graders and eighth-graders increased between 1998 and 2002.

• The average scores of 12th-grade male students declined in 2002, but no change was detected in the average scores of 12th-grade female students.

Figure 4. Gaps in average writing scale scores by gender, grades 4, 8, and 12: 1998 and 2002.

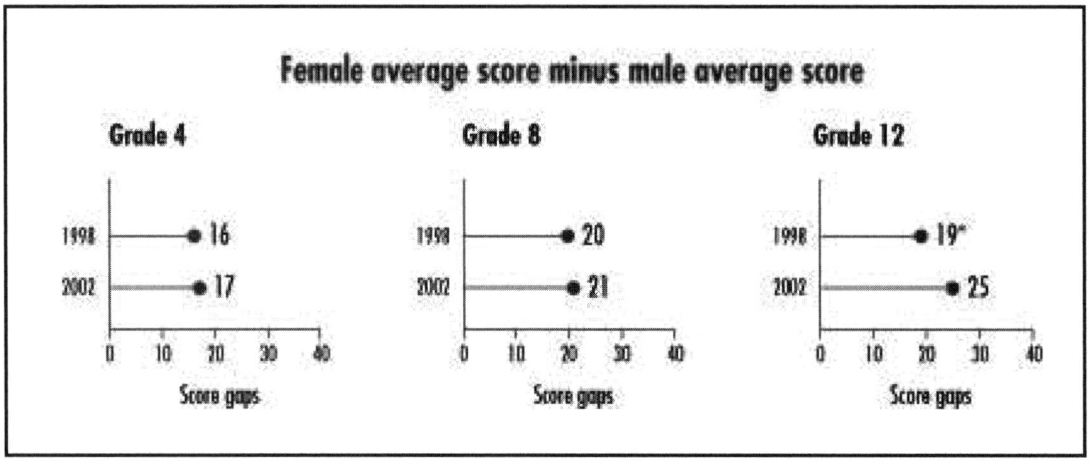

Female average score minus male average score

Grade 4 — 1998: 16, 2002: 17
Grade 8 — 1998: 20, 2002: 21
Grade 12 — 1998: 19*, 2002: 25

* Significantly different from 2002.

Note: Score gaps are calculated based on differences between unrounded average scale scores.

Source: U.S. Department of Education, Institute of Education Sciences, National Center for Education Statistics, *National Assessment of Educational Progress (NAEP),* 1998 and 2002 Writing Assessments.

Major Findings

- In 2002, female students' average writing scale score was higher than male students' by 17 points at grade 4, 21 points at grade 8, and 25 points at grade 12.

- A significant increase in the gap between 12th-grade males and females was detected between 1998 and 2002.

Strategies for Change

After reading the research it is apparent that it would be very helpful to boys if we made some changes in the ways we do things at school and at home. These strategies are organized by two areas: school (behaviors, reading, and writing) and home.

Strategies for Changes at School

Behaviors

- Provide all students with opportunities to move frequently, especially during lessons.

- Provide boys with opportunities to show off through drama, sharing hobbies and interests, demonstrating something they have read about, etc.

- Allow boys to move about the classroom as they work and think.

- Give boys frequent breaks from work.

- Give boys lots of opportunity for sensory activities and experiences.

Reading

- Make sure that classroom and school libraries have print materials that will interest boys.

- Provide boy-friendly culminating activities after completing books.

- Provide a *Guinness Book of World Records* in the classroom and several in the library.

- Separate participants in literature circles and book discussion groups by gender.

- Do NOT make students read out loud unless they have had time to prepare.

- Use readers' theater for developing fluency.

- NEVER use round robin reading.

- Demonstrate how to read and enjoy nonfiction.

- Read humorous poetry aloud.

- Feature booktalks on nonfiction books.

- Introduce nonfiction authors just as you would feature authors of fiction.

- Have a male teacher sponsor a book club with middle school boys—it's a guy thing.

- Establish a program where all the males in the school read aloud regularly to classes.

- Be accepting of the reading needs of boys.

- Give reluctant readers short passages to read.

- After or even before boys read about something, allow them to do it, to experience it.

- Invite fathers and male community figures to be guest readers in the classroom.

- On career day, ask guests to tell what they have to read in order to succeed in their jobs.

- Take advantage of free or inexpensive books offered through books clubs and offer books as prizes.

- Read nonfiction books aloud.

- Use retelling as a way to check comprehension.

- Use art as a way to respond to literature.

- Abandon standard comprehension in favor of student questions and logical discussion questions.

- Use graphic organizers to help boys understand their reading.

- Model quality responses to literature.

- Conduct frequent interest inventories to help boys find appropriate books and to put boys with similar interests together in book discussion groups.

- Be sure to give boys some prior knowledge before they begin to read a book.

- Boys need to have successful reading experiences.

- Provide more titles similar in theme to the one a boy has selected or one read aloud and enjoyed.

- Always allow choice in book selection.

- Do not think of comic books or graphic novels as sub-literature.

- Provide boys with a buddy reading program.

Writing

- Accept the writing styles of boys—blood, guts, crashes, aliens, etc.; acceptance of such topics may help a boy to become more comfortable with the writing process.

- Encourage boys to read movie scripts and to read about movie and theater production and then have them write plays.

- Encourage boys to draw their thoughts first before they write, if they prefer.

- Make writing a natural extension of reading through journaling and reflections where comments, feelings, questions, etc., can be written about what students have read.

Strategies for Changes for Parents

- Provide a wide variety of reading materials in the home.

- Encourage fathers to become active in their sons' reading.

- Encourage all adult males at home to share their reading preferences.

- Model reading.

- Set aside a daily time when everyone reads—turn off the TV, the video games, and the computer.

- Read to/with kids long after the lower elementary grades.

- Have reading parties for kids (Harry Potter, Boxcar Children, Lemony Snicket, Redwall, etc.).

- Purchase books or bookstore gift cards for gifts for kids' friends.

- Rewards kids with trips to the book store/library.

- Take advantage of any special kids' programs at the local public library.

- Before or after seeing a movie with kids, read the book version together and then compare and contrast the two versions.

- Provide a wide variety of response activities to books.

- Read the newspaper with boys.

- Support reading selections—never ridicule.

- Always allow choice in book selection.

- Do not think of comic books or graphic novels as sub-literature.

The following is a plan to change the school culture with regard to reading. The suggestions involve all members of the school community; some will require some fund-raising, and all are favorable to providing a positive reading experience for boys especially.

Whole School Reading Plan

- Read Aloud—at least once a week—with all members of the school community (especially the males) serving as readers and featuring nonfiction titles in each classroom or by grade level group.

- Drop Everything and Read (DEAR)—15 minutes a day, every day, perhaps alternating classes, subject areas, or time periods, and all students should have a personal selection reading time as part of homework.

- Media Center Reading Environment—conducive to boys: chess and other games, a wide variety of magazines, nonfiction titles focusing on current male interests, and graphic novels; students act as consultants and help select books and magazines for the media center.

- Classroom Reading Environment—reading area with special seating, books available, attention to a wide variety of titles, and media incorporated within all content areas, time to read, time to talk about books.

- Web Page—page for media center where students post reviews and the media specialist can introduce new titles, promotions, general information, lists of links of interest to boys.

- Publishing Center—where writers can produce books for peers and younger students.

- Book Clubs—for teachers to read and discuss current literature, for students to get together to all read one title or one author or on one subject and then share ideas and thoughts on their readings; for parents, students, by gender, grade levels—offer a father–son or mother–son book club in the library or after school/before school by classroom.

- Curriculum Changes—to include literature in all content areas, encouraging all content area teachers to teach reading strategies, to encourage all teachers to use nonfiction and picture books, teach students how to read nonfiction and feature nonfiction authors, and to allow students time to read.

- More Curriculum Changes—to help traditional English literature teachers include fiction to compare and contrast with classics, to emphasize students responding to literature on a personal level through literature circles and response journals, to explore reading workshops in which students select their own reading material and work at their own pace and in which skill teaching is done on an as-needed basis.

- Visual Literacy—students should be taught to gather information and construct their own charts, graphs, and diagrams, they need instruction in organizing large amounts of information—with special training in the use of a wide variety of graphic organizers; students also need to be taught skimming, scanning, note taking, and summarizing.

- Special Events—connecting music and literature with plays, meaningful field trips, older students reading to and writing for younger students and vice versa, author and illustrator visits, author of the year focus for the entire school.

- Booktalks—librarians, teachers, and students all sharing a brief and tantalizing glimpse of excellent titles to promote recreational reading.

- Professional Development—sending teachers to reading conferences and workshops, opportunities to visit schools and libraries with good reading programs, memberships in professional reading organizations, professional libraries with lots of good books on reading, and professional journals for reading and discussion at faculty meetings.

- State-sponsored Reading Programs—Florida has Sunshine State Young Readers Award—students read from a short list and vote on their favorite titles.

- Bookshare—circulation of used books—kids bring in old books and buy back others for 50 cents each; teachers can have copies for classroom libraries, and the leftovers can be donated to local charities.

1

Humor

Introduction

Some of the most successful stories for boys have been the slapstick, silly stories about taboo subjects that seem to have an unusual effect on boys. The more silly it is the more they like it. They like to read riddle books and joke books, they love puns. The more off-the-wall the humor is, the more they enjoy it. They delight in comic books and therefore any book written in a comic book format. They like silly illustrations. Books in which pranks and mayhem reign are their favorites. They find forbidden topics like bathroom humor to be the funniest.

Discussion Questions

- What makes this story funny?

- Is the humor at the expense of someone's feelings?

- If there are illustrations, do they add to the humor?

- If this is a joke book, have you shared any of the jokes with your friends?

- Would this story make a good movie?

- Are the characters believable or just too silly?

- Is there anything unusual about the format of the book? If so, why is it appealing?

Annotations

Herbert, Solomon J., and George H. Hill. *Bill Cosby.* **Chelsea House Publishers, 1999. ISBN: 0-7910-1121-6. Gr. 4-7**

Bill Cosby grew up in North Philadelphia and was the eldest of four boys. His father was unable to support the family and eventually stopped coming around. His mother worked long hours as a domestic and it was up to Bill to keep his brothers out of trouble. Much of his comic material comes from those difficult growing-up years. Bill was an outstanding athlete and student and liked to make people laugh. He started as a stand-up comic in his second year at Temple University and began the hardest and most difficult thing he could do, break into show business. Nonfiction.

Hiaasen, Carl. *Hoot.* **Alfred A. Knopf, 2002. ISBN: 0-375-82181-3. Gr. 5 & up**

Roy noticed a boy running down the street barefoot one day, when he was on the bus going to a new school. This was the first thing of interest to Roy since he had moved to Florida, so he made several inquiries. At the same time, a piece of property was to become the new Mother Paula's All-American House of Pancakes, that is if they can stop the vandalism long enough to begin bulldozing the property. Roy learns that the barefoot boy, Mullet Fingers, is the one who is causing the delays, hoping to discourage the property owners, in order to save the threatened burrowing owls.

Korman, Gordon. *Son of the Mob.* **Hyperion Paper, 2004. ISBN: 0-7868-1593-0. YA**

Seventeen-year-old Tony Luca's family is in the "vending machine business," and his father is king of the mob. Tony disassociates himself from the crime organization but the "family" interferes with his life. Tony is thrown into jail when it is discovered that the Porsche he received for his 16th birthday is "hot." He meets Kendra and falls in love but soon discovers that her father is an FBI agent—actually he is *the* FBI agent who is bugging and wiretapping the family house. In the end, Tony is successful at being part of his family, preserves his self-respect, keeps his conscience clear, and maintains his relationship with Kendra.

Middleton, Haydn. *Roald Dahl: An Unauthorized Biography.* **Heinemann Library, 1999. ISBN: 1-57572-693-9.**

British children's author Roald Dahl led as exciting a life as those he wrote about. He has been described as a big child, one who relates well to children. He shares their sense of humor and manifests it in books such as *Matilda, The BFG,* or *The Witches.* Nonfiction.

Morgenstern, Susie. *A Book of Coupons.* **Viking, 2001. ISBN: 0-670-89970-4. Gr. 3-6**

It was the first day of school and the kids were expecting a young teacher this year. Instead an old, fat, wrinkly man walked into class, and the first thing he did was hand each student a book of coupons. These coupons were unique, for example: sleep late one day, forget your homework, or skip a day of school. He also compared himself to Santa and gave them lessons for a year, books, and everything life had taught him. Monsieur Noel gets into trouble with Incarnation Perez, the principal, for his undisciplined ways. Eventually Incarnation Perez has her way, and Monsieur Noel's contract is not renewed. At the end-of-the-year party, Monsieur Noel admires those who have used up their coupons and compares using the coupons to the fact that when you are born you have a whole book of coupons to use. In the end, the children give him a coupon for a well-deserved retirement.

Morris, Gerald. *The Ballad of Sir Dinadan.* **Houghton Mifflin, 2003. ISBN: 0-618-19099-6. Gr. 5-9**

The original Arthur stories were sung by minstrels or troubadours. In this tale, Dinadan is a lesser-known knight who would rather sing his ballad than fight. After his father forces him to be a knight, he leaves and wanders around, living up to the code of knighthood in a subtle way as opposed to fellow knights who seek recognition and self-fulfillment, disregarding the knight's code of honor. Through Dinadan's adventures, we meet Tristram, who tells everyone of his vow of silence because his true love is married to another. We are also introduced to Cullogh, who performs ridiculous tasks or trials with hopes of winning a bride. Humble Dinadan, in his own quiet way, is a more honorable knight than either Tristram or Cullogh.

Paulsen, Gary. *Harris and Me.* **Harcourt Brace, 1993. ISBN: 0-15-292877-4. Gr. 4-7**

A young boy is placed with some distant relatives on a farm for the summer. It will be the first time that the young boy will experience love and a family. He immediately becomes fast friends with Harris, and together they get into numerous hilarious adventures.

Pilkey, Dav. *The Adventures of Super Diaper Baby.* **Scholastic Press, 2002. ISBN: 0-439-37605-X. Gr. 2-5**

Super Diaper Baby is born and immediately has a run-in with Deputy Dangerous and his dog. Deputy Dangerous seeks revenge, and his dog rescues Super Diaper Baby and becomes the future Diaper Dog. Together they get rid of Deputy Dangerous, and all live happily ever after.

Sachar, Loius. *Holes.* **Farrar, Straus & Giroux, 1998. ISBN: 0-374-33265-7. Gr. 5 & up**

Stanley Yelnats IV's great-grandfather lost his entire fortune and a curse was placed on his descendants. Our Stanley continues to have bad luck. He is sent to Camp Green Lake for a crime he didn't commit. Camp Green Lake is not at all what its name suggests: It is desolate and barren with no water in sight, so fences and guards are unnecessary. His punishment is to dig a hole five feet by five feet in width and depth every day in the hot sun before he is allowed to do anything else. Everything changes when Stanley finds a small gold tube with the initials KB on it. Won the Newbery Award in 1999.

Scieszka, Jon. *The Good, the Bad, and the Goofy.* **Penguin Putnam Books for Young Readers, 1992. ISBN: 0-670-84380-6. Gr. 4-7**

The Time Warp Trio of Joe, Sam, and Fred are drawn to the magical book and go back in time to the days of cowboys and the Wild West. They narrowly miss a stampede, learn how to ride drag or round up stray horses, and meet up with the Cheyenne Indians along with Custer and his Seventh Cavalry. The trio save Black Kettle and his people, work their magic, and then are gone.

Snicket, Lemony. *The Bad Beginning.* **HarperCollins, 1999. ISBN: 0-06-051828-6. Gr. 4-7**

This is the first book in the series, A Series of Unfortunate Events. The author warns the reader that this is a book without a happy ending. The three Baudelaire youngsters are wealthy orphans after their parents perish in a fire that destroys their home. The executor of the will sends them to live with Count Olaf, a distant relative who treats them cruelly. Count Olaf is an actor, who schemes to take their money by including the children in a play and marrying the oldest girl, Violet. If the children do not comply, Count Olaf threatens to kill the baby. Clever Violet saves the situation, but Count Olaf escapes to plan more treachery.

Stauffacher, Sue. *Donuthead.* **Random House, 2003. ISBN: 0-375-82468-5. Gr. 3-7**

Fifth-grader Franklin Delano Donuthead believes that one side of his body is shorter than the other, and just to be sure, he measures both sides every day. Donuthead has many fears, both imagined and real. He worries about disasters, germs, and Marvin Howerton, captain of the basketball team. Franklin is paired up with Sarah, a new student at school. When Marvin begins to talk trash to Donuthead, Sarah leaps up and breaks his nose. From that moment on Franklin develops a relationship with Sarah, and with intervention on his mother's part, Sarah's dreams are fulfilled and Donuthead learns what it is like to be fearless.

Tolan, Stephanie. *Surviving the Applewhites.* **HarperCollins Juvenile Books, 2002. ISBN: 0-06-623602-9. Gr. 5 & up**

Jake Semple is a juvenile delinquent who has recently been thrown out of another school. He ends up at the Applewhite's home school, Creative Academy, on their farm, called Wit's End. Each of the Applewhites is unique. The only normal one is their daughter E. D., who tries to set up a curriculum and keep the home schooling organized. Jake first resists their attempts to include him, but eventually he gets drawn into Mr. Applewhite's little theater presentation of *The Sound of Music,* which is staged in the barn.

Bibliography

Anderson, M. T. *Burger Wuss.* Candlewick Paper, 1999. ISBN: 0-7636-1567-6. Gr. 7-10

Ardagh, Philip. *Dreadful Acts.* Holt, 2003. ISBN: 0-8050-7155-5. Gr. 4-7

———. *A House Called Awful End.* Holt, 2002. ISBN: 0-8050-6828-7. Gr. 4-7

Brooke, William J. *A Is for AARRGH!* HarperCollins, 1999. ISBN: 0-06-023394-X. Gr. 5-8

Byars, Betsy. *Bingo Brown's Guide to Romance.* Puffin Paper, 2000. ISBN: 0-14-036080-8. Gr. 5-8

Corbet, Robert. *Fifteen Love.* Walker, 2003. ISBN: 0-8027-8851-3. Gr. 7-10

Cottonwood, Joe. *Babcock.* Scholastic Paper, 1996. ISBN: 0-590-22221-X. Gr. 7-10

Dahl, Roald. *Matilda.* Puffin Paper, 1998. ISBN: 0-14-130106-6. Gr. 4-8

———. *The Umbrella Man and Other Stories.* Viking, 1998. ISBN: 0-670-87854-5. Gr. 8-12

Daldry, Jeremy. *The Teenage Guy's Survival Guide: The Real Deal on Girls, Growing Up, and Other Guy Stuff.* Little, Brown Paper, 1999. ISBN: 0-316-17824-1. Gr. 6-9

Delaney, Michael. *Deep Doo-Doo and the Mysterious E-mail.* Dutton, 2001. ISBN: 0-525-46530-8. Gr. 5-7

Doyle, Roddy. *The Giggler Treatment.* Scholastic, 2001. ISBN: 0-439-16300-5. Gr. 2-5

Ferris, Jean. *Love Among the Walnuts.* Harcourt, 1998. ISBN: 0-15-201590-6. Gr. 7-10

Fiedler, Lisa. *Lucky Me.* Clarion, 1998. ISBN: 0-395-89131-0. Gr. 6-10

Fleischman, Sid. *Disappearing Act.* HarperCollins, 2003. ISBN: 0-06-051963-0. Gr. 4-6

Frank, Lucy. *The Annoyance Bureau.* Simon & Schuster, 2002. ISBN: 0-689-84903-6. Gr. 5-8

Freeman, Martha. *Fourth Grade Weirdo*. Random House, 2001. ISBN: 0-440-41689-2. Gr. 3-5

Friedman, Robin. *How I Survived My Summer Vacation: And Lived to Write the Story*. Front Street, 2000. ISBN: 0-8126-2738-5. Gr. 5-9

Gantos, Jack. *Jack Adrift: Fourth Grade without a Clue*. Farrar, Straus & Giroux, 2003. ISBN: 0-374-39987-5. Gr. 4-7

Gorman, Carol. *Dork on the Run*. HarperCollins, 2002. ISBN: 0-06-029410-8. Gr. 4-7

Hayes, Daniel. *Flyers*. Simon & Schuster, 1996. ISBN: 0-689-80372-9. Gr. 8-12

Henry, Chad. *DogBreath Victorious*. Holiday, 1999. ISBN: 0-8234-1458-2. Gr. 6-10

Howe, Norma. *Blue Avenger Cracks the Code*. Holt, 2000. ISBN: 0-8050-6372-2. Gr. 7-12

Jennings, Richard W. *My Life of Crime*. Houghton, 2002. ISBN: 0-618-21433-X. Gr. 4-8

Korman, Gordon. *No More Dead Dogs*. Hyperion, 2001. ISBN: 0-7868-2462-X. Gr. 5-7

———. *This Can't Be Happening at MacDonald Hall*. Scholastic, 1990. ISBN: 0-590-44213-9. Gr. 4-7

———. *Don't Care High*. Scholastic Paper, 1986. ISBN: 0-590-40251-X. Gr. 7-10

Kurzweil, Allen. *Leon and the Spitting Image*. Greenwillow Books, 2003. ISBN: 0-06-053930-5. Gr. 4-6

Lubar, David. *Wizards of the Game*. Philomel, 2003. ISBN: 0-399-23706-2. Gr. 6-8

Lynch, Chris. *Extreme Elvin*. HarperCollins, 1999. ISBN: 0-06-028210-X. Gr. 8-10

———. *Slot Machine*. HarperCollins, 1995. ISBN: 0-06-023585-3. Gr. 8-10

Mackay, Claire, selector. *Laughs*. Tundra Paper, 1997. ISBN: 0-88776-393-6. Gr. 5-8

Mason, Simon. *The Quigleys at Large*. Random House, 2003. ISBN: 0-385-75031-5. Gr. 4-6

Mills, Claudia. *Alex Ryan, Stop That!* Farrar, Straus & Giroux, 2003. ISBN: 0-374-34655-0. Gr. 4-7

———. *You're a Brave Man, Julius Zimmerman*. Farrar, Straus & Giroux, 1999. ISBN: 0-374-38708-7. Gr. 5-7

Nodelman, Perry. *Behaving Bradley*. Simon & Schuster, 1998. ISBN: 0-689-81466-6. Gr. 8-10

Palatini, Margie. *The Web Files*. Hyperion, 2001. ISBN: 0-7868-2366-6. Gr. 6-8

Paulsen, Gary. *The Schernoff Discoveries*. Delacorte, 1997. ISBN: 0-385-32194-5. Gr. 4-8

Payne, C. D. *Revolting Youth: The Further Journals of Nick Twisp*. Aivia Press, 2000. ISBN: 1-882647-15-7. Adult

———. *Youth in Revolt: The Journals of Nick Twisp*. Broadway Books, 1996. ISBN: 0-385-48196-9. Adult

Peck, Richard. *A Long Way from Chicago*. Dial, 1998. ISBN: 0-8037-2290-7. Gr. 6-10

———. *A Year Down Yonder*. Dial, 2000. ISBN: 0-8037-2518-3. Gr. 6-10

Pinkwater, Daniel M. *The Hoboken Chicken Emergency*. Simon & Schuster, 1999. ISBN: 0-689-82889-6. Gr. 3-6

————. *Looking for Bobowicz: A Hoboken Chicken Story.* HarperCollins, 2004. ISBN: 0-06-053554-7. Gr. 3-6

Pullman, Philip. *I Was a Rat: Or the Scarlet Slippers.* Random House, 2002. ISBN: 0-440-41661-2. Gr. 4-7

Sachar, Louis. *Dogs Don't Tell Jokes.* Sagebrush Education Resources, 1997. ISBN: 0-7857-0133-8. Gr. 5-8

————. *There's a Boy in the Girl's Bathroom.* Random House, 1997. ISBN: 0-676-76236-0. Juv

Scrimger, Richard. *Noses Are Red.* Tundra, 2002. ISBN: 0-88776-610-2. Gr. 4-7

Smallcomb, Pam. *The Last Burp of Mac McGerp.* Bloomsbury Children's Books, 2003. ISBN 1-58234-856-1. Juv

Smith, Edwin R. *Blue Star Highway, Vol. 1: A Tale of Redemption from North Florida.* Mile Marker Twelve Publishing Paper, 1997. ISBN: 0-9659054-0-3. Gr. 7-12

Smith, Greg Leitich. *Ninjas, Piranhas and Galileo.* Little, Brown, 2003. ISBN: 0-316-77854-0. Gr. 5-8

Snicket, Lemony. *The Carnivorous Carnival.* HarperCollins, 2002. ISBN: 0-06-029640-2. Gr. 4-8 (See others in the series.)

Spinelli, Jerry. *Space Station Seventh Grade.* Little, Brown Paper, 2000. ISBN: 0-316-80605-6. Gr. 6-8

————. *Who Put That Hair in My Toothbrush.* Sagebrush Education Resources, 1994. ISBN: 0-8085-7233-4. Gr. 5-8

Strasser, Todd. *Girl Gives Birth to Own Prom Date.* Simon & Schuster, 1996. ISBN: 0-689-80482-2. Gr. 7-10

Trembath, Don. *A Fly Named Alfred.* Orca Paper, 1997. ISBN: 1-55143-083-5. Gr. 7-10

Van Draanen, Wendelin. *Shredderman: Attack of the Tagger.* Knopf, 2004. ISBN: 0-375-82352-2. Gr. 2-5

————. *Shredderman: Meet the Gecko.* Random House, 2005. ISBN: 0-375-82353-0. Gr. 2-5

————. *Shredderman: Secret Identity.* Knopf, 2004. ISBN: 0-375-82351-4. Gr. 2-5

Weeks, Sarah. *Guy Time.* HarperCollins, 2000. ISBN: 0-06-028366-1. Gr. 5-7

Weston, Martha. *Act I, Act II, Act Normal.* Millbrook, 2003. ISBN: 0-7613-1779-1. Gr. 4-7

Wibberley, Leonard. *The Mouse That Roared.* Buccaneer, 1992. ISBN: 0-89966-887-9. Gr. 7-12

Nonfiction

Fleischman, Sid. *The Abracadabra Kid: A Writer's Life.* Greenwillow Books, 1996. ISBN: 0-688-14859-X. Gr. 6-12

Schuman, Michael A. *Charles M. Schultz: Cartoonist and Creator of Peanuts.* Enslow, 2002. ISBN: 0-7660-1846-6. Gr. 6-10

————. *Bill Cosby: Actor and Comedian.* Enslow, 1995. ISBN: 0-89490-548-1. Gr. 6-12

Spinelli, Jerry. *Knots in My Yo-Yo String: The Autobiography of a Kid.* Knopf, 1998. ISBN: 0-679-98791-6. Gr. 5-8

Picture Books

Alexander, Lloyd. *The Fortune-Tellers.* Dutton Children's Books, 1992. ISBN: 0-525-44849-7 Juv

Browne, Anthony. *Willy's Pictures.* Candlewick, 2000. ISBN: 0-7636-1323-1. Gr. 5-8

Dahl, Roald. *Roald Dahl's Revolting Rhymes.* Random House, 2002. ISBN: 0-375-81556-2. Juv

Goble, Paul. *Iktomi and the Ducks: A Plains Indians Story.* Scholastic, 1993. ISBN: 0-531-07044-1. Juv

Macaulay, David. *Motel of the Mysteries.* Houghton Mifflin, 1979. ISBN: 0-395-28425-2. Gr. 7 & up

McDermott, Gerald. *Zomo the Rabbit: A Trickster Tale from West Africa.* Harcourt, 1992. ISBN: 0-15-299967-1. Juv

Pilkey, Dav. *Dogzilla.* Harcourt, 1993. ISBN: 0-15-223945-6. Juv

———. *Kat Kong.* Harcourt, 1993. ISBN: 0-15-242037-1. Juv

Raschka, Chris. *Arlene Sardine.* Orchard, 1998. ISBN: 0-531-30111-7. Juv

Scieszka, Jon. *The Stinky Cheese Man and Other Fairly Stupid Tales.* Viking, 1992. ISBN: 0-670-84487-X. Juv

———. *The True Story of the 3 Little Pigs by A. Wolf.* Viking, 1989. ISBN: 0-670-82759-2. Juv

Seuss, Dr. *Oh, the Places You'll Go.* Random House, 1993. ISBN: 0-679-84736-7. Juv

Smith, Lane. *The Happy Hocky Family.* Viking, 1993. ISBN: 0-670-85206-6. Juv

Steig, William. *C D B?* Simon & Schuster, 2003. ISBN: 0-689-85706-3. Juv

Trivizas, Eugene. *The Three Little Wolves and the Big Bad Pig.* Simon & Schuster, 1993. ISBN: 0-689-50569-8. Juv

Wiesner, David. *Tuesday.* Houghton Mifflin, 1991. ISBN: 0-395-55113-7. Juv

Annotated Journal Article

Gantos, Jack. "Smart, Sensitive & Out of Control: A Writer Turns His Attention to Kids Who Have a Tough Time Staying on Task." *School Library Journal* **(April 2001): 63-64.**

Gantos discusses children with ADHD, his experiences with them, and how many of his main characters demonstrate the same characteristics of children who are smart but still have a hard time staying on task.

Adventure

Introduction

Adventure stories have always been favorites of boys; the more thrilling and daring the plot, the better. Climbing mountains, battling snakes and alligators, rafting the white rapids, and swimming in shark-infested waters create page-turning excitement for boys. These stories usually have strong main characters who are fearless, brave, and always heroic. They are aggressive and can survive the most incredible circumstances.

Discussion Questions

- What makes this book exciting?

- Can you imagine yourself having similar adventures?

- Could this story actually happen?

- Do you know anyone who is like the main character?

- If you were the main character, would you have done anything differently?

Annotations

Allende, Isabel. *City of the Beasts.* **HarperTrophy, 2004. ISBN: 0-06-053503-2. Gr. 5 & up**

Fifteen-year-old Alex is sent to live with his unconventional grandmother while his mother undergoes chemotherapy treatment. Alex and his grandmother become part of an International Geographic expedition up the Amazon River to locate the legendary creature, the Beast. Alex meets Nadia, the daughter of the guide, and together they are called upon to save the indigenous People of the Mist living in Eye of the World. It is here that they see the Beasts who are the Gods and protectors of memory for the People of the Mist. The Beasts would on occasion kill a foreigner, and because of this their legend has grown, drawing attention to the area, which in turn jeopardizes the isolation of the Indians. Alex tries to convince the Beasts that the only way they and the people will survive is if all the Beasts remain hidden and secure in the mountain while the People of the Mists permit some contact with those outsiders who only seek to help them. Alex and Nadia bargain with the Beasts: If they do what the Beasts ask of them, Nadia requests the three magnificent eggs she had seen in a vision and Alex asks for the water of health for his mother. As Alex and Nadia complete the tasks of the Beasts, next they have to ensure that greedy adventurers are prohibited from entering the Eye of the World, wiping out the Indian population, and taking all of its wealth and resources.

Cadnum, Michael. *Blood Gold.* **Viking, 2004. ISBN: 0-670-05884-X. Juv**

One could not help but like Ezra in spite of his leaving Elizabeth behind with child while he seeks gold in the West. William, who is a good friend of Elizabeth, departs for San Francisco by way of the Isthmus of Panama with the idea of informing Ezra about Elizabeth's condition. Along the way, William encounters many adventures, and it seems that William is not the only one looking for Ezra. Red-haired Murray, with two companions, is just ahead of William, and he is not the kind of person one wants as an enemy. The closer William gets to the gold fields the more distracted he becomes by all the potential wealth and the attention of a certain young lady. William knows immediately that something is wrong when he arrives at Spanish Bar, the camp of Ezra. Murray has already been there, and now William is following the man who murdered Ezra and is leaving a trail of blood.

Chambers, Aldan. *Postcards from No Man's Land.* **Dutton Books, 1999. ISBN: 0-525-46863-3. YA**

Jacob Todd travels to Amsterdam, in place of his grandmother, to attend a ceremony honoring his grandfather and other soldiers who liberated Holland from Germany in World War II. Young Jacob meets the dying Geertrui, who hid his injured grandfather, Jacob, and learns how he died before the war ended. Geertrui reveals a secret she has kept all these years. She had relations with the grandfather and had a child from the relationship. Geertrui has lived this lie long enough and unburdens her soul to young Jacob in narratives revealing both the past and present.

Cowley, Joy. *Hunter.* **Philomel Books, 2004. ISBN: 0-399-24227-9. YA**

A New Zealand Maori slave boy named Hunter seeks freedom from his cruel captors but risks all to help Marama, a girl with blond hair, and her two younger brothers. The story is told in alternating chapters and reaches across 200 years. Hunter's escape in 1805 and Marama and her siblings' survival of a small airplane crash in the same location in 2005. Hunter, who sees into the future, guides Marama in her thoughts and helps her to survive until rescued, at great personal risk to himself and his new freedom.

Cummings, Pat, and Linda Cummings. *Talking with Adventurers.* **National Geographic Society, 1998. ISBN: 0-7922-7068-1. Gr. 4-7**

All of the 12 adventurers interviewed love their work and face many obstacles and hardships along the way. They describe how they became "interested in the subject that became a life's work," and they each answer the same 10 questions. Included are the following adventurers: Christina M. Allen (rain forest ecologist), Robert Ballard (explorer), Michael L. Blakey (anthropologist), Ann Bowles (bioacoustician), David Doubilet (underwater photographer), Jane Googall (ethologist), Dereck & Beverly Joubert (wildlife filmmakers), Michael Novacek (paleontologist), Johan Reinhard (anthropologist), Rick C. West (arachnologist), and Juris Zarins (archaeologist). Nonfiction.

Funke, Cornelia. *The Thief Lord.* **Scholastic, 2002. ISBN: 0-439-40437-1. Gr. 4-7**

Prosper and his younger brother, Bo, run away to Venice to escape from their aunt and uncle. Esther, the aunt, is only interested in keeping Bo and tries to separate the brothers. The boys meet Hornet, Ricco, Mosco, and the mysterious Scipio or thief lord. Young Scipio watches over the other orphans and brings them objects to sell. They stay in an abandoned movie theater, watch out for each other, and become a family. Will Scipio achieve his dream of aging and escaping his father? Will Prosper rescue Bo from aunt Esther, and who becomes the new thief lord?

Gourley, Catherine, ed. *Read for Your Life: Tales of Survival from the Editors of Read Magazine.* **Millbrook Paper, 1998. ISBN: 0-7613-0344-8. Gr. 5-8**

"*Read* is a literature magazine published for students in middle and senior high school." This book includes 10 stories of survival and courage that first appeared in *Read* magazine. The stories are divided into three sections; ordinary heroes, bad luck or bad judgment, and survival of the fittest.

Hobbs, Will. *Wild Man Island.* **HarperCollins, 2002. ISBN: 0-380-73310-2. Gr. 6 & up**

Andy sneaks away from his kayak group in search of Hidden Falls, the location where his father, an archeologist, died. Andy thought that he could visit the falls and then return to camp in time for the float plane that was scheduled to pick up the group. Returning to the camp, Andy is caught in a gale and is forced to land on the Fortress of the Bears or Admiralty Island. Trying to survive, Andy locates an abandoned canning factory and briefly encounters a wild man. Andy asks for help, and the man leaves a spear and flint knife for his protection. A Newfoundland dog is attracted to the smells from the spear and leads Andy to the wild man's survivalist lodgings. Andy has an opportunity to leave the island with the wildlife biologists, who are there to trap the wild man's dog so it doesn't mate with the newly arrived wolves. Knowing what the biologists are planning to do, Andy escapes and warns the wild man of their plans. Together they escape the island, each with his own plans for the future.

Horowitz, Anthony. *Eagle Strike.* **Penguin, 2004. ISBN: 0-399-23979-0. YA**

Teenage spy Alex Rider was visiting his girlfriend, Sabina, in south France when he spied the assassin Yassen Gregorovich on a large yacht. Yassen attempted to kill Sabina's father. Alex, on his own, follows Yassen and learns that he is working for the famous, well-respected pop singer Damian Cray. Why is Damian Cray hiring an assassin, and what are his plans that require the use of a flash drive that cost $2 million? The adventures begin with Alex fighting in a bull fight, a high-speed bicycle chase, and participating in a live video game with possibly deadly consequences.

Martel, Yann. *Life of Pi: A Novel.* **Harcourt, 2002. ISBN: 0-15-100811-6. Adult**

Sixteen-year-old Pi survives a ship sinking and spends seven months on a life boat with a Bengal tiger. By helping Richard Parker, the royal Bengal tiger, to survive, Pi also survives to reach land in Mexico. Pi is questioned further by some officials, who do not believe his story, so he tells another story, more gruesome and horrible. Neither story can be proved, so all agree that the story with animals is the better story and it remains part of the official report.

Mikaelsen, Ben. *Touching Spirit Bear.* **HarperCollins, 2001. ISBN: 0-380-97744-3. Gr. 5-9**

Cole Matthews is a bully with so much anger inside that he viciously beats a ninth-grade classmate until he has brain damage. Cole faces a prison sentence but instead is offered an alternative, Circle Justice. This is based on Native American tradition; Cole is banished, alone, to a remote Alaskan island for a year. Cole has an encounter with a Spirit bear and is badly mauled and left for dead. After finally being rescued, he spends six months recovering from his injuries, and during that time he realizes he must control his anger and change his ways.

Naidoo, Beverley. *The Other Side of Truth.* **HarperCollins, 2000. ISBN: 0-06-029628-3. Gr. 5 & up**

Sade and Femi witness their mother's death in Nigeria. Their father, a reporter, is threatened because of his outspoken opinions. Sade and Femi are smuggled illegally to London and have many frightening experiences when the uncle they are supposed to stay with mysteriously disappears.

Rees, Celia. *Pirates!* **Bloomsbury, 2003. ISBN: 1-58234-816-2. Gr. 7-10**

Nancy Kingdom inherited her father's Jamaican plantation in the early 18th century. Her deceitful brother promises her in marriage to a cruel and domineering neighbor, Bartholomew, the Brazilian. When Nancy learns of the plot, she escapes into the mountains with Minerva Sharpe, a slave from her plantation. At the first opportunity, the girls leave the island and join a pirate ship. They have many experiences in the Caribbean waters and along the African coast. Sometimes they disguise themselves as men; at other times they remain in women's clothes to confuse potential victims. The Brazilian continues to follow their exploits and uses Minerva in a cruel manner to lure and take Nancy into custody. This time the Brazilian is planning to kill Nancy and the rest of the pirate rabble.

Taylor, Theodore. *The Cay.* **Random House, 1987. ISBN: 0-385-07906-0. Gr. 5 & up**

After the Germans torpedo the freighter on which Phillip and his mother are traveling from wartime Curacao to the United States, Phillip finds himself dependent on Timothy, an old, black West Indian sailor. Shipwrecked, there are just the two of them. This is the story of their struggle for survival and of Phillip's efforts to adjust to his new disability, blindness, and to understand the dignified, wise, and loving old man who is his companion.

Bibliography

Aiken, Joan. *Midwinter Nightingale.* Delacorte, 2003. ISBN: 0-385-73081-0. Gr. 5-8

Alexander, Lloyd. *The Gawgon and the Boy.* Dutton, 2001. ISBN: 0-525-46677-0. Gr. 5-7

Ashby, John. *Sea Gift.* Clarion, 2003. ISBN: 0-395-77603-1. Gr. 5-8

Avi. *The Christmas Rat.* Simon & Schuster, 2002. ISBN: 0-689-83842-5. Gr. 4-7

Bedard, Michael, selector. *The Painted Wall and Other Strange Tales.* Tundra, 2005. ISBN: 0-88776-652-8 Gr. 4-6

Bell, Hilari. *Flame: The Book of Sorahb.* Simon & Schuster, 2003. ISBN: 0-689-85413-7. Gr.7-10

Bernardo, Anilu. *Jumping Off to Freedom.* Arte Publico Paper, 1996. ISBN: 1-55885-088-0. Gr. 7-10

Bodett, Tom. *Williwaw.* Random, 1999. ISBN: 0-375-80687-3. Gr. 5-8

Browne, N. M. *Warriors of Camlann.* Bloomsbury, 2003. ISBN: 1-58234-817-0. Gr. 7-10

Cadnum, Michael. *Forbidden Forest: The Story of Little John and Robin Hood.* Orchard, 2002. ISBN: 0-439-31774-6. Gr. 7-10

Carbone, Elisa. *The Pack.* Viking Children's Books, 2003. ISBN: 0-670-03619-6. Gr. 7-9

Cole, Brock. *The Goats.* Farrar, Straus & Giroux, 1987. ISBN: 0-374-42575-2. Gr. 6-9

Coleman, Michael. *Weirdo's War.* Orchard Paper, 1998. ISBN: 0-531-30103-6. Gr. 5-8

Colfer, Eoin. *Artemis Fowl: The Eternity Code.* Hyperion, 2003. ISBN: 0-7868-1914-6. Gr. 5-9

Collins, Suzanne. *Gregor the Overlander.* Scholastic, 2003. ISBN: 0-439-43536-6. Gr. 4-7

Cottonwood, Joe. *Quake!* Scholastic, 1995. ISBN: 0-614-32018-6. Gr. 5-8

Cussler, Clive. *Inca Gold.* Archway Paper, 1998. ISBN: 0-671-02056-0. Adult

———. *Shock Wave.* Pocket Books Paper, 1999. ISBN: 0-671-02055-2. Adult

De Guzman, Michael. *Melonhead.* Farrar, Straus & Giroux, 2002. ISBN: 0-374-34944-4. Gr. 5-8

Dumas, Alexandre. *Count of Monte Cristo.* Random, 1996. ISBN: 0-679-60199-6. Gr. 8-12

Dygard, Thomas J. *River Danger.* Morrow, 1998. ISBN: 0-688-14852-2. Gr. 5-9

Ellis, Sarah. *The Several Lives of Orphan Jack.* Groundwood, 2003. ISBN: 0-88899-529-6. Gr. 7-10

Fama, Elizabeth. *Overboard.* Cricket, 2002. ISBN: 0-8126-2652-4. Gr. 4-8

Ferris, Jean. *All That Glitters.* Farrar, Straus & Giroux, 1996. ISBN: 0-374-30204-9. Gr. 7-10

Gee, Maurice. *The Fat Man.* Simon & Schuster, 1997. ISBN: 0-689-81182-9. Gr. 8-10

George, Jean Craighead. *Tree Castle Island.* HarperCollins, 2002. ISBN: 0-06-000255-7. Gr. 4-7

Gilbert, Barbara Snow. *Paper Trail.* Front Street, 2000. ISBN: 1-886910-44-8. Gr. 7-12

Haddix, Margaret Peterson. *Among the Betrayed.* Simon & Schuster, 2002. ISBN: 0-689-83905-7. Gr. 7-10

Hausman, Gerald. *Castaways: Stories of Survival.* Greenwillow Books, 2003. ISBN: 0-06-998598-3. Gr. 5-8

———. *Tom Cringle: The Pirate and the Patriot.* Simon & Schuster, 2001. ISBN: 0-689-82811-X. Gr. 6-8

Hesse, Karen. *Stowaway.* Simon & Schuster, 2000. ISBN: 0-689-83987-1. Gr. 5-8

Hobbs, Will. *Down the Yukon.* HarperCollins, 2001. ISBN: 0-06-029540-6. Gr. 5-8

———. *Far North.* Morrow, 1996. ISBN: 0-688-14192-7. Gr. 7-12

———. *Jason's Gold.* Morrow, 1999. ISBN: 0-688-15093-4. Gr. 5-9

Horowitz, Anthony. *Skeleton Key.* Philomel, 2003. ISBN: 0-399-23777-1. Gr. 7-10

Jacques, Brian. *Castaways of the Flying Dutchman.* Philomel, 2001. ISBN: 0-399-23601-5. Gr. 6-10

Jordan, Sherryl. *The Hunting of the Last Dragon.* HarperCollins, 2002. ISBN: 0-06-028902-3. Gr. 8-12

Karr, Kathleen. *Bone Dry.* Hyperion, 2002. ISBN: 0-7868-0776-8. Gr. 5-8

Kehret, Peg. *Earthquake Terror.* Puffin Paper, 1998. ISBN: 0-14-038343-3. Gr. 4-7

Korman, Gordon. *Shipwreck.* Scholastic, 2001. ISBN: 0-439-16456-7. Gr. 4-6

Marsden, John. *Burning for Revenge.* Houghton Mifflin, 2000. ISBN: 0-395-96054-1. Gr. 7-12

Mazer, Harry. *Snow Bound.* Delacorte, 1987. ISBN: 0-8446-6240-2. Gr. 5-7

McCaughrean, Geraldine. *Gilgamesh the Hero.* Eerdmans, 2003. ISBN: 0-8028-5262-9. Gr. 4-6

Miklowitz, Gloria. *Camouflage.* Harcourt, 1998. ISBN: 0-15-201467-5. Gr. 8-10

Morpurgo, Michael. *Kensuke's Kingdom.* Scholastic, 2003. ISBN: 0-439-38202-5. Gr. 4-7

Myers, Edward. *Climb or Die: A Test of Survival.* Hyperion, 1994. ISBN: 0-7868-1129-3. Gr. 4-8

———. *Survival of the Fittest.* Montemayor, 2000. ISBN: 0-9674477-2-0. Gr. 5-8

Naylor, Phyllis Reynolds. *The Fear Place.* Aladdin, 1994. ISBN: 0-689-80442-3. Gr. 4-6

Neale, Jonathan. *Lost at Sea.* Houghton Mifflin, 2002. ISBN: 0-618-13920-6. Gr. 6-9

Nolan, Peggy. *The Spy Who Came in from the Sea.* Pineapple, 1999. ISBN: 1-56164-186-3. Gr. 4-8

Osterweil, Adam. *The Amulet of Komondor.* Front Street, 2003. ISBN: 1-886910-81-2. Gr. 5-8

Parkinson, Curtis. *Storm-Blast.* Tundra Paper, 2003. ISBN: 0-88776-630-7. Gr. 4-8

Paulsen, Gary. *Brian's Hunt.* Random House, 2003. ISBN: 0-385-74647-4. Gr. 6-9

———. *Brian's Winter.* Delacorte, 1996. ISBN: 0-385-32198-8. Gr. 5-9

———. *The River.* Delacorte, 1991. ISBN: 0-385-30388-2. Gr. 5-10

———. *White Fox Chronicles: Escape, Return, Breakout.* Delacorte, 2000. ISBN: 0-385-32254-2. Gr. 6-9

Petersen, P. J. *Rising Water.* Simon & Schuster, 2002. ISBN: 0-689-84148-5. Gr. 6-12

Philbrick, Rodman. *The Young Man and the Sea.* Blue Sky Press, 2004. ISBN: 0-439-36829-4. Juv

Richardson, V. A. *The House of Windjammer: Book One.* Bloomsbury, 2003. ISBN: 1-58234-811-1. Gr. 7-12

Rodda, Emily. *Rowan and the Ice Creepers.* HarperCollins, 2003. ISBN: 0-06-029781-6. Gr. 4-6

Rottman, S. L. *Rough Waters.* Peachtree Publishers, 1998. ISBN: 1-56145-172-X. Gr. 8-10

Salisbury, Graham. *Shark Bait.* Bantam Paper, 1997. ISBN: 0-440-22803-4. Gr. 7-12

Smith, Roland. *Thunder Cave.* Hyperion, 1995. ISBN: 0-78868-1159-5. Gr. 5-8

Springer, Nancy. *Lionclaw.* Putnam, 2002. ISBN: 0-399-23716-X. Gr. 5-8

Strasser, Todd. *Shark Bite.* Scholastic Paper, 1998. ISBN: 0-671-023098-8. Gr. 5-8

————. *Thief of Dreams.* Putnam, 2003. ISBN: 0-399-23135-8. YA

Taylor, Theodore. *Rogue Wave and Other Red-Blooded Sea Stories.* Harcourt, 1996. ISBN: 0-15-201408-X. Gr. 6-10

Wallace, Bill. *Skinny-Dipping at Monster Lake.* Simon & Schuster, 2003. ISBN: 0-689-85150-2. Gr. 5-8

Weaver, Bill. *Memory Boy.* HarperCollins, 2001. ISBN: 0-06-028811-6. Gr. 7-10

Whelan, Gloria. *Are There Bears in Starvation Lake?* Random House, 2002. ISBN: 0-307-26515-3. Gr. 3-4

White, Ruth. *Tadpole.* Farrar, Straus & Giroux, 2003. ISBN: 0-374-31002-5. YA

Zindel, Paul. *Night of the Bat.* Hyperion, 2001. ISBN: 0-78868-0340-1. Gr. 6-9

Nonfiction

Alexander, Caroline. *The* Endurance*: Shackleton's Legendary Antarctic Expedition.* Knopf, 1998. ISBN: 0-375-40403-1. Gr. 9 & up

Allen, Thomas B. *Remember Pearl Harbor: American and Japanese Survivors Tell Their Stories.* National Geographic, 2001. ISBN: 0-7922-6690-0. Gr. 4-8

Armstrong, Jennifer. *Shipwreck at the Bottom of the World: The Extraordinary True Story of Shackleton and the* Endurance. Crown, 1999. ISBN: 0-517-80014-4. Gr. 7-12

Calabro, Marian. *The Perilous Journey of the Donner Party.* Clarion, 1999. ISBN: 0-395-86610-3. Gr. 6-9

Goldsmith, Connie. *Lost in Death Valley: The True Story of Four Families in California's Gold Rush.* Twenty-First Century, 2001. ISBN: 0-7613-1915-8. Gr. 5-8

Junger, Sebastian. *The Perfect Storm: True Story of Men against the Sea.* Norton, 1997. ISBN: 0-393-05032-7. Gr. 9 & up

Krakauer, Jon. *Into Thin Air.* Random House, 1998. ISBN: 0-679-46271-6. Gr. 9 & up

Leroe, Ellen. *Disaster! Three Real-Life Stories of Survival.* Hyperion, 2000. ISBN: 0-7868-1403-9. Gr. 4-7

McNab, Chris. *Survive in the Jungle with the Special Forces "Green Berets."* Mason Crest, 2002. ISBN: 1-59084-004-6. Gr. 6-8

Morley, Jacqueline. *How Would You Survive in the American West?* Franklin Watts, 1996. ISBN: 0-531-15308-8. Gr. 4-6

Morris, Deborah. *Teens 911: Snowbound, Helicopter Crash, and Other True Survival Stories.* Health Communications, 2002. ISBN: 0-7573-0039-1. Gr. 7 & up

Murphy, Jim. *Gone A-Whaling: The Lure of the Sea and the Hunt for the Great Whale.* Clarion, 1998. ISBN: 0-395-698472-2. Gr. 7-12

Philbrick, Nathaniel. *In the Heart of the Sea: The Tragedy of the Whaleship* Essex. Penguin, 2001. ISBN: 0-14-100182-8. Gr. 9 & up

————. *Revenge of the Whale: The True Story of the Whaleship* Essex. Putnam, 2002. ISBN: 0-399-23795-X. Gr. 6-10

Picture Books

Base, Graeme. *Animalia.* Harry N. Abrams, 1987. ISBN: 0-8109-1868-4. Juv

Blake, Robert J. *Togo.* Philomel, 2002. ISBN: 0-399-23381-4. Juv

George, Jean Craighead. *Cliff Hanger.* HarperCollins, 2002. ISBN: 0-06-000260-3. Juv

Johnston, Tony. *Sunsets of the West.* Putnam, 2002. ISBN: 0-399-22659-1. Juv

Kimmel, Elizabeth Cody. *Ice Story: Shackleton's Lost Expedition.* Clarion, 1999. ISBN: 0-395-91524-4. Juv

Macaulay, David. *Ship.* Houghton Mifflin, 1993. ISBN: 0-395-52439-3. Gr. 5-9

Martin, Jacqueline Briggs. *The Lamp, the Ice, and the Boat Called* Fish. Houghton Mifflin, 2001. ISBN: 0-618-00341-X. Juv

San Souci, Robert D. *Larger Than Life: The Adventures of American Legendary Heroes.* Harcourt, 2000. ISBN: 0-15-200398-3. Juv

Say, Allen. *Grandfather's Journey.* Houghton Mifflin, 1993. ISBN: 0-395-57035-2. Juv

Sis, Peter. *Follow the Dream: The Story of Christopher Columbus.* Alfred A. Knopf, 2003. ISBN: 0-679-80628-8. Juv

Venables, Stephen. *To the Top: The Story of Everest.* Candlewick Press, 2003. ISBN: 0-7636-2115-3. Gr. 4 & up

Annotated Journal Article

Halls, Kelly. "When Picture Books Grow Up." *BookLinks* **(May 2003): 51-54.**
    Many educators who work with older students use picture books to introduce new topics, start discussion on a topic, or entice reluctant readers. Picture books are not just for kids anymore. They can contain sophisticated humor and plays on words and provide poignant introductions to serious topics. Picture books can also serve as models and give upper elementary and middle school students ideas for creative writing. This article has quotes from Jon Scieszka, Jules Feiffer, and William Steig and also includes an annotated bibliography of good picture books for older readers.

3

Information/Nonfiction

Introduction

Boys like books that are crammed with facts, information, illustrations, diagrams, and photographs that further explain the text. They like their facts in small chunks of text, their information well-organized, and an information book with a thorough index. Boys like amazing and unusual facts—things they can share with their peers. Books that tell them how to do things and provide directions for hands-on experiments and projects are at the top of the list. It is very important to survey their interests so that you can provide nonfiction books that they will love.

Discussion Questions

- How does the information provided in this book compare to or supplement the information in your classroom text?

- What are the most interesting facts you learned in this book?

- How is the information organized? Is it easy to locate what you want?

- Are there clear headings and subheadings to help you navigate through the information?

- Have you read other books on this same topic? If so, how did the other books compare?

- If you could talk to the author of this book, what questions would you ask?

- Will you look for other books on this topic?

Annotations

Drake, Ernest. *Dragonology: The Complete Book of Dragons.* **Candlewick Press, 2003. ISBN: 0-7636-2329-6. Gr. 3 & up**

A scientific fantasy treatment of dragons that includes locations of dragons in the world, different species of dragons, natural history of dragons, working with dragons, and appendices, covering a dragonological laboratory, useful spells and charms, dragonologists and dragonslayers of history, and the work of a dragonologist.

Fritz, Jean. *Leonardo's Horse.* **Putnam, 2001. ISBN: 0-399-23576-0. Gr. 3-6**

This book begins with a brief biography of Leonardo Da Vinci and his desire to make a bronze horse for the Duke of Milan. Leonardo made a clay model of the horse in November 1493 but never completed the project. In 1988, Charles Dent started working on the project that Leonardo never finished with hopes of giving the horse to Italy one day, a present from the American people.

Lessem Don. *Scholastic Dinosaurs A to Z: The Ultimate Dinosaur Encyclopedia.* **Scholastic Reference, 2003. ISBN: 0-439-16591-1. Gr. 4-8**

Dinosaurs lived on the land between 65 and 222 million years ago. Scientists have discovered the remains of about 1,000 different kinds of dinosaurs. This is an alphabetical resource of all known dinosaurs to date. "Each entry includes information about a dinosaur's name, size, age, diet, and physical details and places where its remains were found."

Nelson, Pete. *Left for Dead: A Young Man's Search for Justice for the USS* **Indianapolis. Delacorte, 2002. ISBN: 0-385-72959-6. Gr. 7-9**

Captain Quint in the movie *Jaws* tells the story of the USS *Indianapolis*. It was torpedoed and went down in 14 minutes, and the survivors were attacked by sharks. Scott Hunter was only 11 years old when he saw this movie and wanted to know more. He soon learned that very little had been written about the greatest sea disaster in U.S. naval history. Scott was encouraged to contact the 154 living survivors and have them fill out a questionnaire and share their stories. Through his research and interviews Scott was convinced that Captain McVay was made a scapegoat by the Navy. He was the "only captain to be tried out of approximately 350 captains who lost their ships during the war." The men were in the water five days and four nights before they were spotted by a plane and rescued. Captain McVay committed suicide 23 years after the USS *Indianapolis* went down. Scott Hunter spent five years clearing Captain McVay's name, righting a wrong and rewriting history.

Packard, Mary, ed. *Ripley's Believe It or Not Special Edition 2004.* **Scholastic Inc., 2004. ISBN: 0-439-46553-2. Juv**

Robert Ripley visited 201 countries and featured many of the customs of the people he met in his cartoons when he got home. During the 1930s and 1940s, he received more than a million letters a year. This special edition includes some of his cartoons from the Ripley archive as well as the weirdest, wildest, and most bizarre people in the world in chapters entitled "Let's Party," "Past Tense," "Disorder in the Court," "Against All Odds," "Body Language," "Wild Things," "Wacky Wonders," "Outrageous," "Freaky," and "Odds and Ends."

Platt, Richard. *Crime Scene: The Ultimate Guide to Forensic Science.* **DK Publishing, 2003. ISBN: 0-7894-8891-4. YA**

Forensic science is a science that must be combined with "the knowledge, experience, and intuition of detectives, uniformed police, and civilian experts, and administrators" to be effective. The chapters include "At the Crime Scene," "The Victim," "Human Identification," "The Suspect," "Analysis of Evidence," "Lethal Agents," and "Crimes without Corpses or White-Collar Crimes." Each chapter includes many visuals and compelling information, followed by an actual case study.

———. *D-Day Landings: The Story of the Allied Invasion.* **DK Publishing, 2004. ISBN: 0-7566-0276-9. Juv**

This DK Reader is for the proficient reader. The attractive format with numerous pictures and sidebars documents the events before, during, and after D-Day.

Schyffert, Bea Uusma. *The Man Who Went to the Far Side of the Moon: The Story of* Apollo 11 *Astronaut Michael Collins.* **Chronicle Books, 2003. ISBN: 0-8118-4007-7. Gr. 5 & up**

Michael Collins circles the moon in a small spacecraft while Neil Armstrong and Buzz Aldrin land the lunar module. He circles the moon 14 times and is out of communication for 48 minutes each time he is on the far side. This is a creative documentary of his experience with photos, diagrams, personal notes, and interesting facts.

Yolen, Jane, and Heidi Elisabet Yolen Stemple. *Roanoke: The Lost Colony: An Unsolved Mystery from History.* **Simon & Schuster, 2003. ISBN: 0-689-82321-5. Juv**

In 1857, 92 colonists left England for the new world: 60 men, 20 women, and 12 children. The previous colonists at Roanoke were not prepared and had had problems with the Native Americans, so they returned to England. Soldiers remained behind at the fort in anticipation of the new group of colonists. When the new group arrived, led by John White, no soldiers were around, only a single skeleton. The newly arrived colonists had not planned on staying in Roanoke, but there was no other option. White was pressured to go back to England to get supplies and soldiers. When he returned three years later the colony was empty and the colonists gone. The authors propose five common theories of what might have happened and leave it up to the reader to draw their own conclusions or propose a new theory. Look for clues throughout the book.

Bibliography

Alabisco, Vincent. *Flash! The Associated Press Covers the World.* Abrams, 1998. ISBN: 0-8109-2793-4. Adult

Ancona, George. *Murals: Walls That Sing.* Marshall Cavendish, 2003. ISBN: 0-7614-5131-5. Gr. 5-8

Ash, Russell. *Great Wonders of the World.* Eyewitness Books, 2000. DK Paper, 2000. ISBN: 0-7894-6505-1. Gr. 4-7

———. *The Top 10 of Everything.* DK Ink, 2003. ISBN: 0-7894-9659-3. YA

———. *Top 10 Quiz Book.* DK Ink, 1998. ISBN: 0-7894-1022-2. Juv

Beatty, Scott. *Batman: The Ultimate Guide.* DK, 2001. ISBN: 0-7894-7865-X. Gr. 6-8

———. *Superman: The Ultimate Guide.* DK, 2002. ISBN: 0-7894-8853-1. Gr. 6-12

Beecroft, Simon. *Super Humans: A Beginner's Guide to Bionics.* Milbrook, 1998. ISBN: 0-7613-0621-8. Gr. 4-6

Berger, Melvin, and Guilda Berger. *Mummies of the Pharaohs: Exploring the Valley of the Kings.* National Geographic, 2001. ISBN: 0-7922-7223-4. Gr. 4-7

Blackburn, Ken. *The World Record Paper Airplane Book.* Workman, 1994. ISBN: 1-56305-631-3. Adult

Blacklock, Dyan. *Olympia: Warrior Athletes of Ancient Greece.* Walker, 2004. ISBN: 0-8027-8790-8. Gr. 2-5

Branzei, Sylvia. *Grossology: The Science of Really Gross Things.* Addison-Wesley Longman, 1998. ISBN: 0-201-40964-X. Juv

Cefrey, Holly. *Backstage at a Music Video.* Children's, 2003. ISBN: 0-516-24324-1. Gr. 5-8

Claybourne, Anna, et al. *The Usborne Book of the Paranormal.* EDC, 2000. ISBN: 0-7460-3390-7. YA

Colman, Penny. *Corpses, Coffins, and Crypts: A History of Burial.* Henry Holt, 1997. ISBN: 0-8050-5066-3. Gr. 4-7

———. *Toilets, Bathtubs, Sinks, & Sewers: A History of the Bathroom.* Atheneum, 1994. ISBN: 0-689-31894-4. Gr. 5-9

Deem, James M. *Bodies from the Bog.* Houghton Mifflin, 2003. ISBN: 0-618-35402-6. Gr. 4-6

DeFalco, Tom. *Hulk: The Incredible Guide.* DK, 2003. ISBN: 0-7894-9771-9. Gr. 6-12

Dewin, Ted. *Inside the Whale and Other Animals.* Scholastic, 1991. ISBN: 0-590-73869-0. Juv

Diehn, Gwen. *Making Books That Fly, Fold, Wrap, Hide, Pop Up, Twist and Turn: Books for Kids to Make.* Lark, 1999. ISBN: 1-57990-023-2. Gr. 3-9

Dorling Kindersley Publishing Staff. *Dorling Kindersley Children's Atlas.* DK Ink, 2000. ISBN: 0-7894-5845-4. Juv

———. *The Ultimate Lego Book: Discover the Lego Universe.* DK Ink, 1999. ISBN: 0-7894-4691-X. Gr. 3-7

Elffers, Joost, and Saxton Freymann. *Play with Your Food.* Michael Friedman, 2002. ISBN: 1-58663-230-2. Juv

Erlbach, Arlene. *The Middle School Survival Guide: How to Survive from the Day Elementary School Ends until the Second High School Begins.* Walker, 2003. ISBN: 0-8027-8852-1. Juv

Farrell, Jeanette. *Invisible Enemies: Stories of Infectious Diseases.* Farrar, Straus & Giroux, 1998. ISBN: 0-374-33637-7. Juv

Fingeroth, Danny. *Backstage at an Animated Series.* Children's, 2003. ISBN: 0-516-24323-4. Gr. 4-8

Fogle, Bruce. *The New Encyclopedia of the Dog.* DK Ink, 2000. ISBN: 0-7894-6130-7. YA

Franco, Betsy. *You Hear Me? Poems and Writing by Teenage Boys.* Turtleback, 2001. ISBN: 0-606-21538-7. YA

Gilford, Clive, et al. *1000 Years of Famous People.* Kingfisher, 2002. ISBN: 0-7534-5540-4. Gr. 6-10

Hampton, Wilborn. *Meltdown: A Race Against Nuclear Disaster at Three Mile Island: A Reporter's Story.* Candlewick, 2001. ISBN: 0-7636-0715-0. Gr. 7 & up

Hansen, Ole Steen. *The Wright Brothers and Other Pioneers of Flight.* Crabtree, 2003. ISBN: 0-7787-1200-1. Gr. 4-7

Hickam, Homer H., Jr. *Rocket Boys: A Memoir.* Dell, 2000. ISBN: 0-385-33321-8. Adult

Imes, Rick. *Incredible Bugs: An Eye-Opening Guide to the Amazing World of Insects.* DIANE, 2000. ISBN: 0-7881-6985-8. Gr. 4-9

Jackson, Ellen. *The Book of Slime.* Millbrook, 1997. ISBN: 0-7613-0042-2. Gr. 2-4

Jukes, Mavis. *The Guy Book: An Owner's Manual: Maintenance, Safety, and Operating Instructions for Boys.* Knopf, 2002. ISBN: 0-679-89028-9. Gr. 7 & up

Kallen, Stuart A. *The History of Rock and Roll.* Gale, 2002. ISBN: 1-59018-126-3. Gr. 6-10

Lauber, Patricia. *The True-or-False Book of Cats.* National Geographic Society, 2001. ISBN: 0-7922-6694-3. Juv

Lawlor, Laurie. *Where Will This Shoe Take You? A Walk Through the History of Footwear.* Walker, 1996. ISBN: 0-8027-8434-8. Gr. 5 & up

Macaulaly, David. *Building Big.* Houghton, 2004. ISBN: 0-618-46527-8. YA

———. *Mosque.* Houghton, 2003. ISBN: 0-618-24034-9. Gr. 4-6

———. *The New Way Things Work.* Houghton, 1998. ISBN: 0-395-93847-3. Gr. 7 & up

Magnuson, Karen. *Fire in Their Eyes: Wildfires and the People Who Fight Them.* Harcourt, 1999. ISBN: 0-15-201042-4. Juv

Malam, John. *Gladiator: Life and Death in Ancient Rome.* DK, 2002. ISBN: 0-7894-8531-1. Gr. 4-8

Masof, Joy. *Oh, Yuck! The Encyclopedia of Everything Nasty.* Workman Publishing, 1999. ISBN: 0-7611-0771-1. Gr. 3-7

McClafferty, Carla Killough. *The Head Bone's Connected to the Neck Bone: The Weird, Wacky, and Wonderful X-Ray.* Farrar, Straus & Giroux, 2001. ISBN: 0-374-32908-7. Juv

McWhirter, Norris. *Norris McWhirter's Book of Historical Records.* Sterling Publishing, 2001. ISBN: 1-85227-894-3. Adult

Montgomery, Sy. *The Man-Eating Tigers of Sundarbans.* Houghton Mifflin, 2001. ISBN: 0-618-07704-9. Gr. 4-6

———. *The Snake Scientists.* Houghton Mifflin, 2001. ISBN: 0-618-11119-0. Gr. 4-6

Morpurgo, Michael, comp. *The Kingfisher Book of Great Boy Stories: A Treasury of Classics from Children's Literature.* Kingfisher, 2000. ISBN: 0-7534-5320-7. Gr. 4-8

Morse, Jenifer Corr. *Scholastic Book of World Records 2005.* Scholastic, 2004. ISBN: 0-439-64935-8. Gr. 4-7

Nicholson, John. *Fishing for Islands: Traditional Boats and Seafarers of the Pacific.* Allen & Unwin, 2002. ISBN: 1-86448-587-6. Gr. 3-8

Parsons, Jayne. *Tornadoes and Other Dramatic Weather Systems.* DK Ink, 2001. ISBN: 0-7894-7980-X. Juv

Platt, Richard. *Eureka: Great Inventions and How They Happened.* Kingfisher, 2003. ISBN: 0-7534-5580-3. Gr. 4-6

Pringle, Laurence. *Sharks! Strange and Wonderful.* Boyds Mills Press, 2001. ISBN: 1-56397-209-3. Juv

Reynolds, David West. *Star Wars: Incredible Cross Sections.* DK Publishing, 1999. ISBN: 0-7894-3480-6. Juv

Richie, Jason. *Space Flight: Crossing the Last Frontier.* Oliver, 2002. ISBN: 1-881508-77-3. Gr. 5-9

Rogers, Kirsteen, et al. *The Usborne Internet-Linked Science Encyclopedia with 1,000 Recommended Web Sites.* Sagebrush Education Resources, 2003. ISBN: 0-613-86942-7. Gr. 3-6

Rubin, Susan Goldman. *Degas and the Dance: The Painter and the Petits Rats, Perfecting Their Art.* Harry N. Abrams, 2002. ISBN: 0-8109-0567-1. Juv

Sandler, Martin W. *Photography: An Illustrated History.* Oxford, 2002. ISBN: 0-19-512608-4. Gr. 6-12

Scamander, Newt. *Fantastic Beasts and Where to Find Them.* Sagebrush Education Resources, 2001. ISBN: 0-613-32541-9. Gr. 3-6

Schaefer, A. R. *Forming a Band.* Capstone, 2003. ISBN: 0-7368-2146-5. Gr. 5-8

Schiff, Nancy Rica. *Odd Jobs: Portraits of Unusual Occupations.* Ten Speed Press, 2003. ISBN: 1-58008-457-5. Adult

Simon, Seymour. *Now You See It, Now You Don't: The Amazing World of Optical Illusions.* HarperCollins, 1998. ISBN: 0-688-16152-9. Gr. 3 & up

Singh, Simon. *The Code Book: How to Make It, Break It, Hack It, Crack It.* Random, 2002. ISBN: 0-365-72913-8. Gr. 7-12

Sloheim, James. *It's Disgusting and We Ate It! True Food Facts from Around the World and Throughout History.* Simon & Schuster, 2001. ISBN: 0-689-84393-3. Juv

Suskind, Ron. *A Hope in the Unseen: An American Odyssey from the Inner City to the Ivy League.* Broadway Books, 1999. ISBN: 0-7679-0126-6. Adult

Suzuki, David, and Kathy Vanderlinden. *Eco-Fun: Great Projects, Experiments and Games for a Greener Earth.* Douglas & McIntyre, 2004. ISBN: 1-55054-823-9. Adult

Swanson, Diane. *Animals Eat the Weirdest Things.* Holt, 1998. ISBN: 0-8050-5846-X. Juv

———. *Burp? The Most Interesting Book You'll Ever Read about Eating.* Kids Can Press, 2004. ISBN: 1-55074-599-9. Gr. 4-9

————. *Hmm? The Most Interesting Book You'll Ever Read about Memory.* Kids Can Press, 2004. ISBN: 1-55074-595-6. Gr. 4-9

Tanaka, Shelley. *Graveyards of the Dinosaurs: What It Is Like to Discover Prehistoric Creatures.* Sagebrush Education, 2000. ISBN: 0-613-89734-X. Gr. 4-8

————. *I Was There: Discovering the Iceman.* Scholastic, 1997. ISBN: 0-590-24950-9. Juv

————. *Secrets of the Mummies: Uncovering the Bodies of Ancient Egyptians.* Turtleback, 2001. ISBN: 0-606-20900-X. Juv

VanCleave, Janice. *Janice VanCleave's Scientists Through the Ages.* Wiley Paper, 2003. ISBN: 0-471-25222-0. Gr. 4-7

Vecchione, Patrice. *Truth & Lies: An Anthology of Poems.* Holt, 2001. ISBN: 0-8050-6479-6. Gr. 7-10

Venables, Stephen. *To the Top: The Story of Everest.* Candlewick Press, 2003. ISBN: 0-7636-2115-3. Gr. 4 & up

Young, Jay. *The Art of Science: A Pop-Up Adventure in Art.* DIANE, 1999. ISBN: 0-7567-5831-9. Gr. 7-9

Picture Books

Brandenberg, Jim. *To the Top of the World: Adventures with Arctic Wolves.* Walker, 1995. ISBN: 0-8027-7462-8. Gr. 3 & up

Cherry, Lynne. *The Great Kapok Tree: A Tale of the Amazon Rain Forest.* Harcourt, 2000. ISBN: 0-15-202614-2. Juv

————. *A River Ran Wild: An Environmental History.* Harcourt, 1992. ISBN: 0-15-200542-0. Gr. 1-4

Cone, Molly. *Come Back, Salmon: How a Group of Dedicated Kids Adopted Pigeon Creek and Brought It Back to Life.* Sierra Club, 1992. ISBN: 0-87156-489-0. Juv

Dillon, Leo and Diane. *To Every Thing There Is a Season.* Scholastic, 1998. ISBN: 0-590-47887-7. Juv

George, Jean Craighead. *The Everglades.* HarperCollins, 1995. ISBN: 0-06-021228-4. Juv

Goble, Paul. *Star Boy.* Simon & Schuster, 1991. ISBN: 0-689-71499-8. Juv

Kimmel, Elizabeth Cody. *Ice Story: Shackleton's Lost Expedition.* Clarion Books, 1999. ISBN: 0-395-91524-4. Juv

Larson, Gary. *There's a Hair in My Dirt: A Worm's Story.* HarperCollins, 1998. ISBN: 0-06-019104-X. YA

McDermott, Gerald. *Arrow to the Sun: A Pueblo Indian Tale.* Viking Children's Books, 1974. ISBN: 0-670-13369-8. Juv

Platt, Richard. *Castle Diary: The Journal of Tobias Burgess.* Candlewick, 2003. ISBN: 0-7636-2164-1. Juv

Polacco, Patricia. *Meteor!* Penguin Group, 1996. ISBN: 0-698-11410-8. Juv

Sturges, Philemon. *Bridges Are to Cross.* Penguin Putnam, 1998. ISBN: 0-399-23174-9. Juv

Whatley, Bruce and Rosie Smith. *Whatley's Quest.* HarperCollins, 1995. ISBN: 0-06-025291-5. Gr. 2 & up

Wick, Walter. *A Drop of Water: A Book of Science and Wonder.* Scholastic, 1997. ISBN: 0-590-22197-3. Juv

Willard, Nancy. *A Visit to William Blake's Inn: Poems for Innocent & Experienced Travelers.* Harcourt, 1981. ISBN: 0-15-293822-2. Juv

———. *Pish Posh, Said Hieronymous Bosch.* Harcourt Brace, 1991. ISBN: 0-15-262210-1. Juv

Wood, Douglas. *Old Turtle.* Scholastic, 2001. ISBN: 0-439-32106-9. Juv

Annotated Journal Article

Jones, Jami. "Saving Kids from Despair: How to Provide the Critical Skills Young People Need to Overcome Adversity." ***School Library Journal*** **(August 2003): 46-49.**

Jones addresses resiliency, the ability to bounce back from adversity—a characteristic that some kids have while others sink deeper and deeper into depression. A media specialist can help students in many ways: by booktalking good books, mentoring, providing an easy-to-use framework for research, helping students learn social skills, and assisting them in developing hobbies.

4

Fantasy/Science Fiction

Introduction

Space travel, aliens, and life on other planets all have special meaning for most boys. They can imagine themselves time warping into other galaxies and brandishing laser weapons to triumph over horrible-looking aliens. They can picture life on Mars and exploring barren landscapes in zero gravity. They certainly have been exposed to enough imagery of what all this might be like through movies and video games. Having all this come to life in their imaginations through the pages of a great science fiction novel would allow a boy's courageous spirit to reach new levels. Boys enjoy reading stories like the Redwall series about animals that talk and lead creative lives and whole civilizations of people who live under the subway system in big cities. Sometimes fantasy stories are about time travel and going back or ahead in time and trying to adjust to different ways of life.

Discussion Questions

- Could this story actually happen?

- What makes this book a fantasy?

- If there are illustrations, do they add to the story?

- Would this book make a good movie?

- Have you read other science fiction books? If so, how did this compare?

- Was the main character like you in any way?

- Were there any new ideas in this book that you had not imagined or read about before?

- Was this story possible?

- What made this story difficult to imagine?

- Was it exciting? Did the words allow you to create a clear picture in your mind?

- Would you recommend this book to others? Why or why not?

Annotations

Armstrong, Jennifer, and Nancy Butcher. *The Kindling.* **HarperCollins, 2002. ISBN: 0-06-029411-6. Gr. 7-10**

Seven children have survived a deadly virus that has killed all of the adults in the United States. These children have formed a family comprising Hunter, Teacher, Mommy, Action Figure, Teddy Bear, Baby, and Doll. Every day is a struggle for food, water, and protection. One day, Anchorman, with his mannequin, Bad Guy (represents the virus) appears at their door. He is not a grown-up but taller than Hunter. Whenever Anchorman has something important to say, he holds a picture up to his face. Bad Guy is always restrained or tied to Anchorman, or Angerman, as he is eventually called. Angerman encourages the family to leave their home and travel with him to Washington, D.C., in search of the president of the United States. The first book in this trilogy ends with the family arriving intact in northern Florida. They have reached the ocean after many misadventures, when they notice a grown-up dressed in white, standing on the beach watching them.

Bolme, Edward. *The Steel Throne.* **Wizards, 2002. ISBN: 078-6927-127. YA**

This is the prelude to the Four Winds Saga. The Unspeakable is draining the Emperor's soul. If it succeeds the empire will be ruined. The Emperor fulfills his duty to his family and empire by committing the ultimate sacrifice. Upon passing over to the other side, Emperor Toturi gathers a force around him to open Oblivion's gate and once again passes to his former life. In doing so he allows the ancient and evil Hantei Emperor to slip through as well. Look at the Web site, www.wizards.com.

Bradbury, Ray. *Fahrenheit 451: The Temperature at Which Book Paper Catches Fire, and Burns . . . .* **Ballantine Books, 1987. ISBN: 0-345-34296-8. Adult**

When all the houses were finally fireproofed there was no need for firemen as they were originally thought of. Now their job is to ensure that everyone is happy all the time, and the way to do that is to burn all books and the houses that hide them. Montag likes his job until he meets a young girl named Clarisse, who is not satisfied to know how things are done, but why. He is also affected by a woman who, when surrounded by her kerosene-soaked books, refuses to leave her house and then strikes a kitchen match against the porch railing. Montag, too, has been hoarding books and develops a plan to hide them in firemen's houses, turn in the alarm, and then see the firemen's houses burn. However, Montag, is forced to make life-altering decisions when he answers one last special assignment and the firemen and their burning equipment stop in front of his own house.

Clements, Andrew. *Things Not Seen.* **Philomel Books, 2002. ISBN: 0-399-23626-0. Gr. 6-9**

Ever wonder what it would be like to be invisible? One morning, Bobby wakes up and discovers he is invisible. Now he cannot do anything like he did before. His situation becomes complicated when his parents are hospitalized from a car accident. What if this is a permanent situation? Will his life be like this forever? Bobby makes a decision not to wait around for stuff to happen to him. He is going to go out and make the most of his life. Thus begins his relationship with a blind girl, Alicia, who helps Bobby figure out a solution to his invisibility.

Colfer, Eoin. *The Supernaturalist.* **Hyperion, 2004. ISBN: 0-7868-5148-1. Gr. 5 & up**

The supernaturalists are on a mission to destroy as many parasites as they can. It is Stephan's belief that the blue boys are sucking the life out of any human who is in pain just like they did when his mother was dying. Stephan, Moni, and Cosmo spend the nights attending to any accidents or cries for help and they destroy the blue boys before they can complete their work. The problem is the blue boys seem to be increasing in number faster than Stephan and his friends can destroy them. The supernaturalists come to realize that instead of destroying the parasites they are in fact helping them to multiply. They must find a way to destroy them once and for all, but what if they are wrong? What if instead of the blue boys sucking the life forces out of people, they are actually sucking the pain out of the people and making their last moments more peaceful?

Corder, Zizou. *Lionboy.* **Dial Books, 2003. ISBN: 0-8037-2982-0. Gr. 3-6**

Charlie Ashanti has a special gift. He is able to talk with cats, both large and small. One day when he arrives home, his mother's lab is wide open, and the house is dark. His parents have been kidnapped, and Charlie begins an adventure that takes him from London to Paris on a circus sailing ship. While looking for his parents, Charlie attends to the lions and helps them escape. Together they are eluding the enemy in their search for Charlie's parents. This is the first of three books and is to be continued.

Haddix, Margaret Peterson. *Among the Brave.* **Simon & Schuster, 2004. ISBN: 0-689-85794-2. Gr. 3-7**

All third children are illegal, because there is not enough food for the people. The Population Police have taken control of the society, and they are increasing their number in order to seek and destroy all third children. Trey is a third child, and it is up to him to rescue his friends who have been captured by the Population Police. Bravely he joins the dreaded Population Police, flees from a rioting crowd, and drives to the Nazerree prison. He narrowly escapes with his friends and the leader of the Liber or free the third children movement. The adults are terrified of the future, so it is up to the third children to discover the weakness of the Population Police and try to bring them down from within. Will any of Trey's friends join him in this new adventure?

Nix, Garth. *The Seventh Tower: The Fall.* **Scholastic Inc., 2000. ISBN: 0-439-17682-4. Gr. 4-7**

It is up to Tal to look after his family while his father is gone, and thought to be dead by some. Tal must steal a larger Sunstone to become a Chosen and help his ailing mother. Tal climbs the red tower of the castle, through the dark veil, and enters a world of Shield Maidens, Icecarls, and ice ships. The only way back to the castle is to bind himself to Milla in her quest to find a Sunstone. When the two are within sight of the castle, Milla and Tal are surrounded by Shield Maidens and taken to their Crone for judgment. If Tal has not told the truth or tries to practice magic, he will be killed.

Philbrick, Rodman. *The Last Book in the Universe.* **Blue Sky Press, 2000. ISBN: 0-439-08758-9. Gr. 6-9**
> In this future world destroyed by an earthquake, an epileptic teenager, Spaz, is told by gang mates to rob an old man named Ryter. Instead, Spaz makes friends with the old man, and when Spaz learns that his sister is dying, Ryter leads Spaz on a dangerous journey to see his sister.

Shusterman, Neal. *Full Tilt.* **Simon & Schuster Books for Young Readers, 2003. ISBN: 0-689-80374-5. YA**
> Sixteen-year-old Blake is always rescuing his younger brother, Quinn, This time Quinn is in a coma, and it is up to Blake to face the challenges ahead for both of them. Blake and two friends enter a surreal amusement park, where the admittance fee is their soul. To leave the park, one must ride seven rides before dawn. The rides are different for each person because they encompass his or her worst fears, but there is a way off of each ride if the person can figure out how. If Blake survives all seven rides, then he must go on one more ride to save his comatose brother. This ride is the bus ride on which he was the sole survivor when he was seven years old.

Bibliography

Fantasy

Alexander, Lloyd. *The Book of Three.* Dell Paper, 1964. ISBN: 0-440-40702-8. Gr. 5-8

———. *Iron Ring.* Puffin Paper, 1997. ISBN: 0-14-130348-4. Gr.6-9

———. *The Rope Trick.* Dutton, 2002. ISBN: 0-525-47020-4. Gr. 4-7

Allen, Will. *Swords for Hire: Two of the Most Unlikely Heroes You'll Ever Meet.* Centerpunch Paper, 2003. ISBN: 0-9724882-0-0. Gr. 5-8

Almond, David. *Heaven Eyes.* Delacorte, 2001. ISBN: 0-385-32770-6. Gr. 5-8

———. *Kit's Wilderness.* Delacorte, 2000. ISBN: 0-385-32665-3. Gr. 6-9

———. *Skellig.* Delacorte, 1999. ISBN: 0-385-32653-X. Gr. 5-8

Atwater-Rhodes, Amelia. *Hawksong.* Delacorte, 2003. ISBN: 0-385-73071-3. Gr. 7-10

———. *Midnight Predator.* Delacorte, 2002. ISBN: 0-385-32794-3. Gr. 7-9

Avi. *Perloo the Bold.* Scholastic Paper, 1998. ISBN: 0-590-11002-0. Gr. 4-7

Barron, T. A. *The Mirror of Merlin.* Putnam, 1999. ISBN: 0-399-23455-1. Gr. 7-10

———. *The Wings of Merlin.* Philomel, 2000. ISBN: 0-399-23456-X. Gr. 7-10

Bell, Hilari. *Flame.* Simon & Schuster, 2003. ISBN: 0-689-85413-7. Gr. 6-10

———. *The Goblin Wood.* HarperCollins, 2003. ISBN: 0-06-051371-3. Gr. 6-10

Blackwood, Gary. *The Year of the Hangman.* Dutton, 2002. ISBN: 0-525-46921-4. Gr. 6-9

Brooks, Bruce. *Throwing Smoke.* HarperCollins, 2000. ISBN: 0-06-028320-3. Gr. 4-7

Browne, N. M. *Warriors of Alavna.* Bloomsbury, 2002. ISBN: 1-58234-775-1. Gr. 7-10

Calhoun, Dia. *Firegold.* Winslow, 1999. ISBN: 1-890817-10-4. Gr. 7-12

Clement-Davies, David. *Fire Bringer.* Dutton, 2000. ISBN: 0-525-46492-1. Gr. 6-12

———. *The Sight.* Dutton, 2003. ISBN: 0-525-46723-8. Gr. 7-12

Collins, Suzanne. *Gregor the Overlander.* Scholastic, 2003. ISBN: 0-439-43536-6. Gr. 4-6

Coville, Bruce. *Aliens Stole My Body.* Minstrel Books, 1998. ISBN: 0-671-02414-0. Gr. 4-7

———. *Song of the Wanderer.* Scholastic, 1999. ISBN: 0-590-45953-8. Gr. 5-8

———. *The Skull of Truth.* Harcourt, 1997. ISBN: 0-15-275457-1. Gr. 5-7

Coville, Bruce, ed. *Half-Human.* Scholastic, 2001. ISBN: 0-590-95944-1. Gr. 7-10

Dickinson, Peter. *The Tears of the Salamander.* Random, 2003. ISBN: 0-385-73098-5. Gr. 6-9

Divakaruni, Chitra Banerjee. *The Conch Bearer.* Millbrook, 2003. ISBN: 0-7613-1935-2. Gr. 5-8

Downer, Ann. *Hatching Magic.* Simon & Schuster, 2003. ISBN: 0-689-83400-4. Gr. 4-7

Drake, Emily. *The Magickers.* DAW Books, 2001. ISBN: 0-88677-935-9. Gr. 5-6

Duane, Diane. *So You Want to Be a Wizard.* Magic Carpet Books, 2001. ISBN: 0-613-36059-1. Gr. 5-8

———. *Wizard's Holiday.* Harcourt, 2003. ISBN: 0-15-204771-9. Gr. 6-9. (See others in the series.)

Etchemendy, Nancy. *The Power of Un.* Front Street, 2000. ISBN: 0-8126-2850-0. Gr. 4-7

Funke, Cornelia. *Inkheart.* Scholastic, 2003. ISBN: 0-439-53164-0. Gr. 6-12

Garfield, Henry. *Tartabull's Throw.* Simon & Schuster, 2001. ISBN: 0-689-83840-9. Gr. 7-10

Gutman, Dan. *Qwerty Stevens Back in Time with Benjamin Franklin.* Simon & Schuster, 2002. ISBN: 0-689-84553-7. Gr. 4-7

Heneghan, James. *Flood.* Farrar, Straus & Giroux, 2002. ISBN: 0-374-35057-4. Gr. 5-8

Hoeye, Michael. *The Sands of Time.* Putnam, 2002. ISBN: 0-399-23879-4. Gr. 5-8

Hoffman, Mary. *Stravaganza: City of Masks.* Bloomsbury, 2002. ISBN: 1-58234-791-3. Gr. 7-12

———. *Stravaganza: City of Stars.* Bloomsbury, 2003. ISBN: 1-58234-839-1. Gr. 6-10

Holt, David, and Bill Mooney. *Spiders in the Hairdo: Modern Urban Legends.* August House, 1999. ISBN: 0-87483-525-9. Gr. 7-12

Hunter, Erin. *Fire and Ice.* HarperCollins, 2003. ISBN: 0-06-000003-1. Gr. 6-9

Ibbotson, Eva. *The Secret of Platform 13.* Dutton, 1998. ISBN: 0-525-45929-4. Gr. 4-7

Jacques, Brian. *The Angel's Comand: A Tale from the Castaways of the Flying Dutchman.* Putnam, 2003. ISBN: 0-399-23999-5. Gr. 5-9

———. *Loamhedge.* Philomel, 2003. ISBN: 0-399-23724-0. Gr. 5-8

———. *Outcast of Redwall.* Philomel, 1996. ISBN: 0-399-22914-0. Gr. 5-8

Jones, Diana Wynne. *Believing Is Seeing.* Greenwillow Books, 1999. ISBN: 0-688-16843-4. Gr. 6-12

———. *The Merlin Conspiracy.* HarperCollins, 2003. ISBN: 0-06-052318-2. Gr. 6-10

Jordan, Scherryl. *The Hunting of the Last Dragon.* HarperCollins, 2002. ISBN: 0-06-028903-1. Gr. 6-10

Kay, Elizabeth. *The Divide.* Scholastic, 2003. ISBN: 0-439-45696-7. Gr. 5-9

La Fevers, R. L. *The Falconmaster.* Dutton, 2003. ISBN: 0-525-46993-1. Gr. 6-8

Lasky, Kathryn. *Guardians of Ga'Hoole: Book One: The Capture.* Scholastic, 2003. ISBN: 0-439-40557-2. Gr. 4-8

Levitin, Sonia. *The Cure.* Harcourt, 1999. ISBN: 0-15-201827-1. Gr. 6-9

Lowry, Lois. *The Giver.* Houghton, 1993. ISBN: 0-395-64566-2. Gr. 6-9

Lyon, Mary E., ed. *Raw Head and Bloody Bones: African-American Tales of the Supernatural.* Macmillan, 1991. ISBN: 0-684-19333-7. Gr. 5-7

MacHale, D. J. *The Lost City of Fear.* Simon & Schuster, 2003. ISBN: 0-7434-3732-2. Gr. 5-8

Mahy, Margaret. *Alchemy.* Simon & Schuster, 2003. ISBN: 0-689-85053-0. Gr. 7-10

Nicholson, William. *Firesong.* Hyperion, 2002. ISBN: 0-7868-0571-4. Gr. 7-12

Nimmo, Jenny. *Charlie Bone and the Invisible Boy.* Scholastic, 2004. ISBN: 0-439-54526-9. Gr. 4-6

———. *Charlie Bone and the Time Twister.* Scholastic, 2003. ISBN: 0-439-49687-X. Gr. 5-7

———. *Midnight for Charlie Bone.* Scholastic, 2003. ISBN: 0-439-47429-9. Gr. 4-6

Nix, Garth. *Mister Monday.* Scholastic Paper, 2003. ISBN: 0-439-55123-4. Gr. 5-8

———. *Shade's Children.* HarperCollins, 1997. ISBN: 0-06-027325-9. Gr. 7-12

November, Sharyn, ed. *Firebirds: An Anthology of Original Fantasy and Science Fiction.* Putnam, 2003. ISBN: 0-14-250142-5. YA

Oppel, Kenneth. *Sunwing.* Simon & Schuster, 2000. ISBN: 0-689-82674-5. Gr. 5-8

Paolini, Christopher. *Eragon.* Knopf, 2003. ISBN: 0-375-82668-8. Gr. 7-12

Pierce, Tamora. *Squire: Protector of the Small.* Random, 2001. ISBN: 0-679-88916-7. Gr. 6-9

Prue, Sally. *Cold Tom.* Scholastic, 2003. ISBN: 0-439-48268-2. Gr. 4-8

Pullman, Philip. *The Amber Spyglass.* Knopf, 2000. ISBN: 0-679-87926-9. Gr. 7-12

———. *Clockwork.* Scholastic, 1998. ISBN: 0-590-12999-6. Gr. 4-7

———. *The Golden Compass.* Knopf, 1996. ISBN: 0-679-87924-2. Gr. 7-12

———. *The Subtle Knife.* Random, 1997. ISBN: 0-679-87925-0. Gr. 7-12

Rowling, J. K. *Harry Potter and the Chamber of Secrets.* Scholastic, 2003. ISBN: 0-439-55489-6. Juv

———. *Harry Potter and the Goblet of Fire.* Scholastic, 1993. ISBN: 0-439-55490-X. Juv

————. *Harry Potter and the Order of the Phoenix.* Scholastic, 1993. ISBN: 0-439-56761-0. Juv

————. *Harry Potter and the Prisoner of Azkaban.* Scholastic, 2004. ISBN: 0-439-65548-X. Juv

————. *Harry Potter and the Sorcerer's Stone.* Scholastic, 2003. ISBN: 0-439-55493-4. Juv

Sedgwick, Marcus. *The Dark Horse.* Random, 2003. ISBN: 0-385-73054-3. Gr. 5-8

Shusterman, Neal. *Downsiders.* Simon & Schuster, 1999. ISBN: 0-689-80375-3. Gr. 8-12

Sleator, William. *Marco's Millions.* Dutton, 2001. ISBN: 0-525-46441-7. Gr. 5-9

Stroud, Jonathan. *The Amulet of Samarkand.* Hyperion, 2003. ISBN: 0-7868-1859-X. Gr. 6-12

Tolkein, J. R. R. *The Fellowship of the Ring: Being the First Part of the Lord of the Rings.* Houghton Mifflin, 1988. ISBN: 0-395-48931-8. Gr. 7 & up

————. *The Hobbit.* Ballantine, 1999. ISBN: 0-618-00221-9. Juv

————. *The Return of the King: Being the Third Part of the Lord of the Rings.* Houghton Mifflin, 1999. ISBN: 0-618-00224-3. Adult

————. *The Silmarillion.* Houghton Mifflin, 2001. ISBN: 0-618-12698-8. Adult

————. *The Two Towers: Being the Second Part of the Lord of the Rings.* Ballantine, 1999. ISBN: 0-345-91744-8. Adult

Turner, Megan. *The Thief.* Greenwillow Books, 1996. ISBN: 0-688-14627-9. Gr. 5-8

Waugh, Sylvia. *Space Race.* Delacorte, 2000. ISBN: 0-385-32766-8. Gr. 4-8

Yolen, Jane. *Boots and the Seven Leaguers: A Rock-and-Troll Novel.* Harcourt, 2000. ISBN: 0-15-202557-X. Gr. 5-9

————. *Odysseus in the Serpent Maze.* HarperCollins, 2001. ISBN: 0-06-028735-7. Gr. 4-7

Science Fiction

Armstrong, Jennifer. *The Keepers of the Flame.* HarperCollins, 2002. ISBN: 0-06-029411-6. Gr. 7-10

Bell, Hilari. *A Matter of Profit.* HarperCollins, 2001. ISBN: 0-06-029513-9. Gr. 6-10

Blacker, Terence. *The Angel Factory.* Simon & Schuster, 2002. ISBN: 0-689-85171-5. Gr. 6-8

Cart, Michael, ed. *Tomorrowland: Ten Stories about the Future.* Scholastic, 1999. ISBN: 0-590-37678-0. Gr. 6-12

Castro, Adam-Troy. *Spider-Man: Secret of the Sinister Six.* Berkley Paper, 2002. ISBN: 0-7434-4464-7. Gr. 7-12

Clancy, Tom, and Steve Pieczenik. *Virtual Vandals.* Berkley Paper, 1999. ISBN: 0-425-16173-0. Adult

Colfer, Eoin. *Artemis Fowl: The Eternity Code.* Hyperion, 2003. ISBN: 0-7868-1914-6. Gr. 6-9. (See others in the series.)

Cooper, Susan. *Green Boy.* Simon & Schuster, 2002. ISBN: 0-689-84751-3. Gr. 4-8

Coville, Bruce, ed. *Bruce Coville's UFOs*. HarperCollins, 2000. ISBN: 0-380-80257-0. Gr. 4-8

———. *Odder Than Ever*. Harcourt, 1999. ISBN: 0-15-201747-X. Gr. 5-9

Crossley-Holland, Kevin. *At the Crossing Places*. Scholastic, 2002. ISBN: 0-439-26598-3. Gr. 5-8

———. *The Seeing Stone*. Scholastic, 2001. ISBN: 0-439-26326-3. Gr. 4-8

Dickinson, Peter. *A Bone from a Dry Sea*. Random, 1993. ISBN: 0-440-21928-0. Gr. 6-9

DuPrau, Jeanne. *The City of Ember*. Random, 2003. ISBN: 0-375-82273-9. Gr. 5-7

Engdahl, Sylvia Louise. *The Far Side of Evil*. Walker, 2003. ISBN: 0-9027-8848-3. Gr. 6-9

Farmer, Nancy. *The Ear, the Eye, and the Arm*. Orchard, 1994. ISBN: 0-531-08679-8. Gr. 7-10

———. *The House of the Scorpion*. Atheneum, 2002. ISBN: 0-689-85222-3. Gr. 7-10.

Gilmore, Kate. *The Exchange Student*. Houghton, 1999. ISBN: 0-395-57511-7. Gr. 6-9

Goodman, Alison. *Singing the Dogstar Blues*. Viking, 2003. ISBN: 0-670-03610-2. Gr. 7-12

Gutman, Dan. *The Edison Mystery*. Simon & Schuster, 2001. ISBN: 0-689-84124-8. Gr. 4-8

Haddix, Margaret Peterson. *Turnabout*. Simon & Schuster, 2000. ISBN: 0-689-82187-5. Gr. 7-10

Hesse, Karen. *Phoenix Rising*. Holt, 1994. ISBN: 0-8050-3108-1. Gr. 6-8

Hoover, H. M. *Another Heaven, Another Earth*. Tor, 2002. ISBN: 0-8125-6761-7. Gr. 6-9

Hughes, Monica. *The Keeper of the Isis Light*. Simon & Schuster, 1981. ISBN: 0-689-83390-3. Gr. 6-9

Jeapes, Ben. *The Xenocide Mission*. Viking, 2002. ISBN: 0-385-75007-2. Gr. 7-10

Klaus, Annette Curtis. *Alien Secrets*. Bantam Books, 1993. ISBN: 0-440-22851-4. Gr. 5-8

Lawrence, Louise. *The Patchwork People*. Clarion, 1994. ISBN: 0-395-67892-7. Gr. 7-10

Layne, Steven L. *This Side of Paradise*. North Star, 2001. ISBN: 0-9712336-9-1. Gr. 7-10

Lowenstein, Sallie. *Focus*. Lion Stone Paper, 2001. ISBN: 0-9658486-3-9. Gr. 5-9

Lubar, David. *Flip*. Tor, 2003. ISBN: 0-765-30149-0. Gr. 5-8

Mackel, Kathy. *Can of Worms*. HarperCollins, 2000. ISBN: 0-380-97681-1. Gr. 4-7

———. *From the Horse's Mouth*. HarperCollins, 2002. ISBN: 0-06-029415-9. Gr. 5-7

Paulsen, Gary. *The Transall Saga*. Delacorte, 1998. ISBN: 0-385-32196-1. Gr. 7-12

Pierce, Tamora. *Street Magic*. Scholastic Paper, 2001. ISBN: 0-590-39628-5. Gr. 5-9

Pratchett, Terry. *The Bromeliad Trilogy: Truckers, Diggers, and Wings*. HarperCollins, 2003. ISBN: 0-06-009493-1. Gr. 4-6

Read Magazine, ed. *Read into the Millennium: Tales of the Future*. Millbrook, 1999. ISBN: 0-7613-0962-4. Gr. 6-8

Reeve, Philip. *Mortal Engines*. HarperCollins, 2003. ISBN: 0-06-008207-0. Gr. 7-10

Skurzynski, Gloria. *The Clones: The Virtual War Chronologs.* Simon & Schuster, 2002. ISBN: 0-689-84463-5. Gr. 6-9

———. *Virtual War.* Simon & Schuster, 1997. ISBN: 0-689-82425-4. Gr. 6-9

Sleator, William. *Boltzman!* Dutton, 1999. ISBN: 0-525-46131-0. Gr. 5-8

———. *Parasite Pig.* Dutton, 2002. ISBN: 0-525-46918-4. Gr. 7-10

Picture Books

Agee, Jon. *The Incredible Painting of Felix Clousseau.* Farrar, Straus & Giroux, 1990. ISBN: 0-374-43582-0. Juv

Browne, Anthony. *Changes.* Farrar, Straus & Giroux, 2002. ISBN: 0-374-41177-8. Juv

Bunting, Eve. *Night of the Gargoyles.* Clarion Books, 1994. ISBN: 0-395-66553-1. Juv

Joyce, William. *A Day with Wilbur Robinson.* HarperCollins, 1993. ISBN: 0-06-443339-0. Juv

Prelutsky, Jack. *The Dragons Are Singing Tonight.* Greenwillow Books, 1993. ISBN: 0-688-09645-X. Juv

Van Allsburg, Chris. *Ben's Dream.* Houghton Mifflin, 1982. ISBN: 0-395-32084-4. Juv

———. *Jumanji.* Houghton Mifflin, 1981. ISBN: 0-395-30448-2. Juv

———. *The Widow's Broom.* Houghton Mifflin, 1992. ISBN: 0-395-64051-2. Juv

———. *The Wreck of the Zephyr.* Houghton Mifflin, 1983. ISBN: 0-395-33075-0. Juv

———. *The Wretched Stone.* Houghton Mifflin, 1991. ISBN: 0-395-53307-4. Juv

Wiesner, David. *Free Fall.* HarperCollins, 1991. ISBN: 0-688-10990-X. Juv

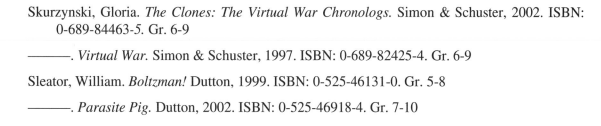

Annotated Journal Article

Odean, Kathleen. "The Story Master: Phillip Pullman." *School Library Journal* (October 2000): 50-54.

This British writer is a superb storyteller. *The Amber Spyglass* is the last of his fantasy trilogy that includes tiny people called Gallivespians, daemons who are spirit companions of people that take animal forms, and includes some themes about the negative power of organized religion. Pullman was once a middle school teacher and did a lot of storytelling of classics with his students. Pullman feels that his fantasy writing is a vehicle for him to explore with his readers what it is like to be a human being and to experience all the things that humans experience in their daily lives.

5

Horror/Mystery

Introduction

A good mystery with lots of clues, cliff-hangers, and puzzles will entertain many boys. They like to be detectives and try to figure out who-done-it. They like suspense and a little intrigue. Boys like to search and dig for facts and try to put the pieces together. Many boys like chilling movies and frightening stories. They like to show how brave and fearless they are or can be. They like stories about ghosts, evil twins, and vampires. The creepier the story is, the better. R. L. Stine's Goosebumps Series proved to be good reads for boys; the covers were always scary even though the story itself wasn't all that bad. The Stine books for teens were much more frightening and menacing.

Discussion Questions

- What makes this book frightening?

- Could the events in this book actually happen?

- If there were illustrations, did they make the story more frightening?

- Was the story believable, or was it just too strange?

- Would you describe this book as a page-turner?

- Would this book make a good movie?

- How does the author grab your interest?

- Are there cliff-hangers? If so, do they entice you to keep reading?

- Was there a good level of suspense in this story?

- Does the author give you enough clues to solve the mystery?

- If you figured out who did it early in the story, were you actually correct in the end?

- Could a movie be made from this book?

- Was the picture on the cover of the book accurate?

Annotations

Anderson, M. T. *Thirsty.* **Candlewick Press, 2003. ISBN: 0-7636-2014-9. Juv**

Chris is noticing some physical changes that he is struggling to control. He is having trouble sleeping and eating. One day, in the woods, he is separated from his friends and meets up with an Avatar of the Forces of Light known as Chet. He tells Chris what he already suspected. With the onset of puberty, Chris will change into a vampire within four months. In this society vampires are hunted and publicly executed. Chet offers to cure Chris of the "scourge of vampirism" if he will act as a spy among the vampires. Chet wants Chris to enter their den, take an object through the gates of the Vampire Lord, activate it, and then leave it behind. This object, the Arm of Moriator, will destroy the Vampire Lord if he tries to escape. Chris agrees to help Chet but he is not sure Chet is telling the truth. Is Chet a celestial being? Is he able to cure Chris?

Atwater-Rhodes, Amelia. *Demon in My View.* **Delacorte, 2000. ISBN: 0-385-32720-X. Gr. 7-12**

Jessica, an author who is a loner at school, is attracted to a new student by the name of Alex. He reminds her of Aubrey, one of the vampire characters from her latest book. Jessica is concerned that the characters in her books are coming to life. How is it that she is able to knowingly write about their past? Without realizing it, Jessica has angered the vampire demons and one in particular by the name of Fala. After a near-death encounter with Fala, Jessica must decide if she to wants to become a vampire, live in their community, and be with Aubrey.

Avi. *Midnight Magic.* **Scholastic, 1999. ISBN: 0-590-36035-3. Gr. 5-9**

Fabrizio is the servant and assistant to Mangus, a magician in the 1400s. Mangus is under house arrest, and his life is spared after he repents being a magician. So why is the king summoning Fabrizio and Mangus to the castle to solve a mystery? Mangus has given up creating the illusion of magic and wants only to speak the truth, but many lives are at stake, including his own.

Brooks, Kevin. *Lucas.* **Scholastic Inc., 2004. ISBN: 0-439-53063-6. Juv**

The Strand connects the island with the mainland at low water. Cait McGann lives on the island with her older brother and father, who is an author of YA books. Cait saw Lucas for the first time on the Strand. She immediately knew that he was different, that Lucas could see beyond things. She only saw Lucas a few times but each time was memorable. The islanders do not like it when they do not know who or what you are. They are suspicious of strangers, and rumors about Lucas abound. Will Cait be able to protect Lucas, and who will protect Cait from Jamie Tait, the local wealthy, lecherous monster?

Crew, Gary. *The Watertower*. Interlink Publishing, 2000. ISBN: 1-56656-331-3. Gr. 2-9

Two boys go up to the water tower for a swim. Spike climbs the ladder first and Bubba, who is afraid of water, follows. After a short time, Bubba decides to leave, only to find his pants missing. Spike offers to run home and get another pair for Bubba. In the meantime Bubba goes back inside to get out of the sun. Something happens to Bubba while Spike is gone. The illustrations, the eyes, and the shape of the water tower provide clues to the strange happenings. Picture book.

Holub, Joseph. *The Robber and Me*. Henry Holt, 1997. ISBN: 0-8050-5599-1. Gr. 3-7

Boniface Schroll, a young orphan, is being delivered to his uncle, the mayor of Graab, a remote village in Germany. The driver abandons Boniface in the middle of the forest with instructions on how to find the village. Boniface is rescued by a strange man who wears a tall black hat. Could he be the Robber Knapp? The townspeople have blamed Robber Knapp for a number of holdups that have taken place, and his children are treated badly. Boniface knows that the Robber Knapp is not the thief, but he doesn't want to jeopardize his struggling relationship with his uncle and thus lose his new home. Will Boniface risk all and tell the truth about Robber Knapp?

Hoobler, Dorothy. *The Ghost in the Tokaido Inn*. Philomel Books, 1999. ISBN: 0-399-23330-X. Gr. 6-8

In 18th-century Japan, 14-year-old Seikei is the son of a tea merchant but aspires to be a samurai. The problem is that one can't just become a samurai; one must be born into it. While on a business trip with his father he witnesses the theft of a costly jewel from an arrogant samurai. He is asked to help find the thief by the famous magistrate, Judge Ooka, and this leads him on a dangerous path of mystery and adventure.

Jacques, Brian. *The Ribbajack & Other Curious Yarns*. Philomel Books, 2004. ISBN: 0-399-24220-1. Gr. 5 & up

"The Ribbajack" is the first of six short stories of horror and mystery. A Ribbajack monster is conjured up in a person's mind and comes alive before midnight to avenge the creator. The greater the evil and hate-filled mind of the creator, the more fearful the Ribbajack. When Archibald Smith conjured up his Ribbajack he directed it to rid the world of the school's chaplain, Reverend Miller. Archibald and his Ribbajack did not know that Reverend Miller was in possession of an ancient charm to ward off and protect him, from such evil. What will be the consequences to the Ribbajack, Archibald Smith, and Reverend Miller when they meet?

Taylor, Theodore. *A Sailor Returns*. Blue Sky Press, 2001. ISBN: 0-439-24879-5. Gr. 5-7

Tom Pentreath has not been in contact with his daughter since her mother died when she was very young. He sends a letter asking if he could come to visit and meet his grandson, Evan. Tom has traveled the world and sailed the seven seas, but he hopes to find peace and make things right with his daughter before he dies. In the process, Tom changes the family for the better.

Zindel, Paul. *The Scream Museum*. Hyperion, 2001. ISBN: 0-7868-1572-8. Gr. 3-7

Peter Christopher (P. C.) Hawke and his friend Mackenzie are in the middle of solving the murder of Dr. Conchetta Farr, head of research at the Museum of Natural History. They know that the accused killer and friend, Tom, was drugged and hypnotized to kill Dr. Farr. The police are satisfied that they have the killer, so it is up to P. C. to find the real killer, and how the Ganesh necklace is involved.

Bibliography

Horror

Atwater-Rhodes, Amelia. *In the Forests of the Night.* Delacorte, 1999. ISBN: 0-385-32674-2. Gr. 7-12

Burgess, Melvin. *The Ghost Behind the Wall.* Holt, 2003. ISBN: 0-8050-7149-0. Gr. 5-7

Cabot, Meg. *Haunted.* HarperCollins, 2003. ISBN: 0-06-029471-X. Gr. 7-10

Carus, Marianne, ed. *That's Ghosts for You: 13 Scary Stories.* Front Street, 2000. ISBN: 0-8126-2675-3. Gr. 4-7

Cray, Jordan. *Gemini 7.* Simon & Schuster, 1997. ISBN: 0-689-81432-1. Gr. 6-10

Duncan, Lois, ed. *Night Terrors: Stories of Shadow and Substance.* Simon & Schuster, 1996. ISBN: 0-689-80346-X. Gr. 6-12

Durant, Alan, ed. *Vampire and Werewolf Stories.* Kingfisher Paper, 1998. ISBN: 0-7534-5152-2. Gr. 5-10

Gorog, Judith. *Please Do Not Touch.* Scholastic Paper, 1995. ISBN: 0-590-46683-6. Gr. 6-12

Hill, Mary, ed. *Creepy Classics: Hair-Raising Horror from the Masters of the Macabre.* Random, 1994. ISBN: 0-679-86692-2. Gr. 6-10

Huntington, Geoffrey. *Sorcerers of the Night.* Regan, 2002. ISBN: 0-06-001425-3. Gr. 7-10

MacDonald, Caroline. *Hostilities: Nine Bizarre Stories.* Scholastic Paper, 1994. ISBN: 0-590-46063-3. Gr. 7-10

Mahy, Margaret, and Susan Cooper. *Don't Read This: And Other Tales of the Unnatural.* Front Street, 1998. ISBN: 1-886910-22-7. Gr. 7-10

McDonald, Joyce. *Shades of Simon Gray.* Delacorte, 2001. ISBN: 0-385-32659-9. Gr. 6-8

McKean, Thomas. *Into the Candlelit Room and Other Strange Tales.* Putnam, 1999. ISBN: 0-399-23359-8. Gr. 6-9

Medearis, Angela Shelf. *Haunts: Five Hair-Raising Tales.* Holiday, 1996. ISBN: 0-7534-5026-7. Gr. 4-7

Morgan, Jill. *Blood Brothers.* HarperCollins Paper, 1996. ISBN: 0-06-440562-1. Gr. 5-8

Murphy, Jim. *Night Terrors.* Scholastic Paper, 1993. ISBN: 0-590-45341-6. Gr. 6-9

Olson, Arielle North, and Howard Schwartz, eds. *Ask the Bones: Scary Stories from Around the World.* Viking, 1999. ISBN: 0-670-87581-3. Gr. 5-9

Patneaude, David. *Dark Starry Morning: Stories of This World and Beyond.* Albert Whitman, 1995. ISBN: 0-8075-1474-8. Gr. 5-8

Pepper, Dennis, ed. *The New Young Oxford Book of Ghost Stories.* Oxford, 1999. ISBN: 0-19-278154-5. Gr. 6-12

Pipe, Jim. *The Werewolf.* Millbrook, 1996. ISBN: 0-7613-0450-9. Gr. 4-7

Price, Susan, ed. *Horror Stories.* Kingfisher Paper, 1995. ISBN: 1-85697-592-4. Gr. 6-12

Rees, Douglas. *Vampire High.* Delacorte, 2003. ISBN: 0-385-73117-5. Gr. 6-9

San Souci, Robert D. *Dare to Be Scared: Thirteen Stories to Chill and Thrill.* Cricket, 2003. ISBN: 0-8126-2688-5. Gr. 4-8

Schreiber, Ellen. *Vampire Kisses.* HarperCollins, 2003. ISBN: 0-06-009334-X. Gr. 7-10

Scott, Kiernan. *Jungle Boy.* Delacorte, 2003. ISBN: 0-385-73113-2. Gr. 6-9

Seabrooks, Brenda. *The Vampire in My Bathtub.* Holiday, 1999. ISBN: 0-8234-1505-8. Gr. 4-7

Shan, Darren. *Cirque Du Freak: A Living Nightmare.* Little, Brown, 2001. ISBN: 0-316-60340-6. Gr. 5-8

———. *Cirque Du Freak: Vampire Mountain.* Little, Brown, 2002. ISBN: 0-316-60806-8. Gr. 5-8.

———. *Tunnels of Blood.* Little, Brown, 2002. ISBN: 0-316-60763-0. Gr. 5-8

Shusterman, Neal. *Scorpion Shards.* Tor Paper, 1996. ISBN: 0-8125-2465-9. Gr. 8-12

Sleator, William. *The Beasties.* Dutton, 1997. ISBN: 0-525-45598-1. Gr. 6-9

Stearns, Michael, ed. *A Nightmare's Dozen: Stories from the Dark.* Harcourt, 1996. ISBN: 0-15-201247-8. Gr. 6-9

Stine, R. L. *The Haunting Hour: Chill in the Dead of Night.* HarperCollins, 2001. ISBN: 0-06-623605-3. Gr. 5-8

Van Belkom, Edo, ed. *Be Afraid! Tales of Horror.* Tundra, 2000. ISBN: 0-88776-496-7. Gr. 8-12

Vande Velde, Vivian. *Being Dead.* Harcourt, 2001. ISBN: 0-15-216320-4. Gr. 7-10

———. *Never Trust a Dead Man.* Harcourt, 1999. ISBN: 0-15-201899-9. Gr. 7-12

Welch, R. C. *Scary Stories for Stormy Nights.* Lowell House Paper, 1995. ISBN: 1-56565-262-2. Gr. 5-7

Mystery

Anderson, Janet S. *The Last Treasure.* Dutton, 2003. ISBN: 0-525-46919-2. Gr. 5-7

Bonners, Susan. *Above and Beyond.* Farrar, Straus & Giroux, 2001. ISBN: 0-374-30018-6. Gr. 5-7

Bowler, Tim. *Storm Catchers.* Simon & Schuster, 2003. ISBN: 0-689-84573-1. Gr. 6-10

Bruchac, Joseph. *Skeleton Man.* HarperCollins, 2001. ISBN: 0-06-029076-5. Gr. 5-9

Christie, Agatha. *Death on the Nile.* Berkley, 2001. (re-issue) ISBN: 0-425-17373-9. Adult

Conrad, Hy. *Whodunit Crime Puzzles.* Sterling Paper, 2002. ISBN: 0-8069-9796-6. Gr. 4-7

Cresswell, Helen. *Mystery Stories: An Intriguing Collection.* Kingfisher Paper, 1996. ISBN: 0-7534- 5025-9. Gr. 8-12

Cross, Gillian. *Phoning a Dead Man.* Holiday, 2002. ISBN: 0-8234-1685-2. Gr. 6-10

DeFelice, Cynthia. *Death at Devil's Bridge.* Farrar, Straus & Giroux, 2000. ISBN: 0-374-31723-2. Gr. 6-10

Doyle, Sir Arthur Conan. *Adventures of Sherlock Holmes.* Avon Paper, 1981. ISBN: 0-380-78105-0. Gr. 7-12

Duncan, Lois. *On the Edge: Stories at the Brink.* Simon & Schuster, 2001. ISBN: 0-689-83256-7. YA

———. *Trapped! Cages of Mind and Body.* Simon & Schuster, 1998. ISBN: 0-689-81335-X. Gr. 7-12

Emerson, Scott. *The Case of the Cat with the Missing Ear: From the Notebooks of Edward R. Smithfield.* Simon & Schuster, 2003. ISBN: 0-689-85861-2. Gr. 5-7

Gaiman, Neil, et al. *Coraline.* HarperCollins Paper, 2004. ISBN: 0-06-057591-3. Gr. 6-8

Gee, Maurice. *The Fat Man.* Simon & Schuster, 1997. ISBN: 0-689-81182-9. Gr. 8-12

Gordon, Lawrence. *Haunted High.* Karmichael Press, 2000. ISBN: 0-9653966-1-4. Gr. 6-9

Gutman, Dan. *Shoeless Joe and Me.* HarperCollins, 2002. ISBN: 0-06-029254-7. Gr. 4-7

Hess, Joan. *Murder@maggody.com: An Arly Hanks Mystery.* Simon & Schuster, 2000. ISBN: 0-684-84563-6. Gr. 10 & up

Heyes, Eileen. *O'Dwyer and Grady Starring in Tough Act to Follow.* Simon & Schuster Paper, 2003. ISBN: 0-689-84920-6. Gr. 4-7

Holm, Jennifer L. *The Creek.* HarperCollins, 2003. ISBN: 0-06-000133-X. Gr. 6-8

Holmes, Barbara Ware. *Following Fake Man.* Knopf, 2001. ISBN: 0-375-81266-0. Gr. 5-8

Honey, Elizabeth. *Remote Man.* Knopf, 2002. ISBN: 0-375-91413-7. Gr. 6-8

Horrowitz, Anthony. *Point Blank.* Putnam, 2002. ISBN: 0-399-23621-X. Gr. 6-10

———. *Stormbreaker.* Philomel, 2001. ISBN: 0-399-23620-1. Gr. 5-9. (See others in the series.)

Jennings, Richard W. *Mystery in Mt. Mole.* Houghton Mifflin, 2003. ISBN: 0-618-28478-8. Gr. 6-9

Konigsburg, E. L. *Silent to the Bone.* Simon & Schuster, 2000. ISBN: 0-689-83601-5. Gr. 5-9

Levin, Betty. *Shadow Catcher.* Greenwillow, 2000. ISBN: 0-688-17862-6. Gr. 4-7

MacPhail, Catherine. *Dark Waters.* Bloomsbury, 2003. ISBN: 1-58234-846-4. Gr. 7-10

McNamee, Graham. *Acceleration.* Random, 2003. ISBN: 0-385-73119-1. YA

Montes, Marisa. *Something Wicked's in Those Woods.* Harcourt, 2000. ISBN: 0-15-202391-7. Gr. 5-7

Murphy T. M. *The Secrets of Code Z.* J. N. Townsend Paper, 2001. ISBN: 1-880158-33-7. Gr. 4-8

Naylor, Phyllis Reynolds. *Bernie Magruder and the Bats in the Belfry.* Simon & Schuster, 2003. ISBN: 0-689-85066-2. Gr. 4-7

Nixon, Joan Lowry. *Ghost Town.* Delacorte, 2000. ISBN: 0-385-32681-5. Gr. 4-7

————. *Playing for Keeps.* Delacorte, 2001. ISBN: 0-385-32759-5. Gr. 6-10

Oates, Joyce Carol. *Freaky Green Eyes.* HarperCollins, 2003. ISBN: 0-06-623759-9. YA

Plum-Ucci, Carol. *The Body of Christopher Creed.* Harcourt, 2000. ISBN: 0-15-202388-7. Gr. 8-12

————. *The She.* Harcourt, 2003. ISBN: 0-15-216819-2. Gr. 8-12

Priestley, Chris. *Death and the Arrow.* Knopf, 2003. ISBN: 0-375-82466-9. Gr. 6-10

Randol, Susan, ed. *Dead Good Read: Classic Tales of Mystery and Horror.* Reader's Digest, 2001. ISBN: 0-7621-0347-7. Gr. 5-9

Roberts, Willo Davis. *The Kidnappers.* Simon & Schuster, 1998. ISBN: 0-689-81394-5. Gr. 4-7

Seidler, Tor. *Brainboy and the Deathmaster.* HarperCollins, 2003. ISBN: 0-06-029181-8. Gr. 4-7

Shan, Darren. *Trials of Death.* Little, Brown, 2003. ISBN: 0-316-60637-8. YA

Singer, Nicky. *Feather Boy.* Delacorte, 2002. ISBN: 0-385-72980-4. Gr. 6-10

Skurzynski, Gloria and Alane Ferguson. *Buried Alive.* National Geographic, 2003. ISBN: 0-7922-6966-7. Gr. 4-7. (See others in the series.)

————. *Deadly Waters.* National Geographic, 1999. ISBN: 0-7922-7037-1. Gr. 4-7

Springer, Nancy. *Blood Trail.* Holiday House, 2003. ISBN: 0-8234-1723-9. YA

Talbert, Marc. *Small Change.* DK Paper, 2000. ISBN: 0-7894-2531-9. Gr. 5-9

Taylor, Theodore. *Lord of the Kill.* Scholastic, 2002. ISBN: 0-439-33725-9. Gr. 6-10

Werlin, Nancy. *Killer's Cousin.* Bantam, 1998. ISBN: 0-385-32560-6. Gr. 7-12

Zindel, Paul. *The Gourmet Zombie.* Hyperion Paper, 2002. ISBN: 0-7868-1590-6. Gr. 6-9

————. *The Phantom of 86th Street.* Hyperion/Volo Paper, 2002. ISBN: 0-7868-1591-4. Gr. 6-9. (See others in the series.)

————. *Rats.* Hyperion, 1999. ISBN: 0-7868-0339-8. Gr. 6-9

————. *The Square Root of Mystery.* Hyperion Paper, 2002. ISBN: 0-7868-1388-4. Gr. 5-7

Nonfiction

Ballinger, Erich. *Detective Dictionary: A Handbook for Aspiring Sleuths.* Lerner, 1994. ISBN: 0-8225-0721-8. Gr. 4-8

Friedlander, Mark P., Jr., and Terry M. Phillips. *When Objects Talk: Solving a Crime with Science.* Lerner, 2001. ISBN: 0-8225-0649-1. Gr. 5-8

Gardner, Robert. *Crime Lab 101: Experimenting with Crime Detection.* Walker, 1992. ISBN: 0-8027-8159-4. Gr. 6-9

Graham, Ian. *Crime-Fighting.* Raintree Steck-Vaughn, 1995. ISBN: 0-8114-3840-6. Gr. 5-8

———. *Fakes and Forgeries.* Raintree Steck-Vaughn, 1995. ISBN: 0-8114-3843-0. Gr. 5-8

Innes, Brian. *Forensic Science.* Mason Crest, 2003. ISBN: 1-59084-373-8. Gr. 6-12

Jackson, Donna M. *The Bone Detectives: How Forensic Anthropologists Solve Crimes and Uncover Mysteries of the Dead.* Little, Brown, 1996. ISBN: 0-316-82935-8. Gr. 5-9

Jones, Charlotte F. *Fingerprints and Talking Bones: How Real Life Crimes Are Solved.* Delacorte, 1997. ISBN: 0-385-32299-2. Gr. 5-8

Larsen, Anita. *Psychic Sleuths.* Macmillan, 1994. ISBN: 0-02-751645-8. Gr. 5-7

Owens, David. *Police Lab: How Forensic Science Tracks Down and Convicts Criminals.* Firefly, 2002. ISBN: 1-55297-620-3. Gr. 6-12

Powell, Phelan. *Major Unsolved Crimes.* Chelsea, 1999. ISBN: 0-7910-4277-4. Gr. 6-9

Wiese, Jim. *Detective Science: 40 Crime-Solving, Case-Breaking, Crook-Catching Activities for Kids.* Wiley Paper, 1996. ISBN: 0-471-11980-6. Gr. 4-7

Yeatts, Tabatha. *Forensics: Solving the Crime.* Enslow, 2001. ISBN: 1-881508-75-7. Gr. 6-9

Picture Books

Base, Graeme. *The Eleventh Hour: A Curious Mystery.* Harry N. Abrams, 1989. ISBN: 0-8109-0851-4. Juv

Van Allsburg, Chris. *The Mysteries of Harris Burdick.* Houghton Mifflin, 1984. ISBN: 0-395-35393-9. Juv

Yolen, Jane. *A Picnic with Piggins.* Harcourt, 1988. ISBN: 0-15-261534-2. Juv

Annotated Journal Article

Stein, Debbie, and Penny Beed. "Bridging the Gap between Fiction and Nonfiction in the Literature Circle Setting." *The Reading Teacher* **(March 2004): 510-518.**
This article provides good information on literature circles, beginning with fiction books. The authors then make a connection between fiction and biography and go on to nonfiction literature circles. They provide a list of companion titles for fiction and nonfiction and some sample worksheets, and they review the importance of discussion and response to literature.

6

Sports

Introduction

Being good at a sport is very important to most boys. In the news today they see the influential lives that many professional athletes lead. Unfortunately, professional athletes are not always good examples. In any case, most boys like sports and want to succeed and be accepted by their peers. Stories that depict the trials and tribulations of those who want to participate help boys to understand that they are not alone in the things they are experiencing. By reading about athletes and different kinds of sports, they can learn statistics, history, terminology, and issues and be more knowledgeable about the topic.

Discussion Questions

- Have you ever played this sport?

- If so, are these experiences similar to any that you have had?

- How important is it to be successful at a sport?

- Did you learn anything new about this sport by reading this book?

- Do you have a better understanding of good sportsmanship?

- Have you read other books on this sport? If so, how were they alike and different?

• Would becoming a professional in this sport be a good career move?

• Is it important to have a college education when you are a professional athlete?

Annotations

Armstrong, Kristin. *Lance Armstrong: The Race of His Life.* **Penguin Putnam, 2000. ISBN: 0-448-42407-X. Gr. 4-7**

Lance Armstrong received his first bike when he was seven. He lived in Plano, Texas, with his mother, who was always by his side. Lance won races all over the United States and went to Italy when he was 18 to train. In his first race in Europe, Lance came in last place. That only made him train harder by riding in the mountains. At 21 Lance Armstrong became the youngest person to win the world championship. Lance continued to win races, including the Tour de France. When he was 25 he discovered that he had a bigger race to win, the race against cancer. Cancer was spreading throughout his body, even to his brain. He was operated on and took cancer-fighting drugs until he was cancer free. Again he started riding and calling teams to take a chance with him. Only the U.S. Postal Service Cycling Team would take a chance with Lance, and he went on to win the Tour de France six times in a row. Nonfiction.

Bauer, Joan. *Sticks.* **Delacorte, 1996. ISBN: 0-385-32165-1. Gr. 3-7**

Fifth-grader Mickey Vernon wants nothing more than to win the youth division of the billiards championship in his New Jersey town. His grandmother owns the pool hall, and his father was a billiards champion before he died, when Mickey was a baby. The defending champ is 13-year-old Buck Pender, the biggest bully in town. Mickey gets some serious coaching from a friend of his dad's and wins the championship despite a sprained wrist.

Carter, Alden R. *Bull Catcher.* **Scholastic Inc., 1997. ISBN: 0-590-50959-4. Gr. 7 & up**

Neil Larsen, nicknamed Bull, starts to think about baseball in November, even though the season doesn't start until April. His best friend Jeff plays shortstop, and Bull is the catcher. They play together in middle school. The book is divided into their four years at Shiply High School. The highlight of every year is the game with Caledonia. Three years in a row they lose the final game of the season. Senior year will be different. It is dedicated to Billy, who died in a tragic car crash. Bull wants to win this championship and final game even though "it was never quite the same after Billy died."

Crutcher, Chris. *Whale Talk.* **HarperCollins, 2001. ISBN: 0-06-029369-1. Gr. 7 & up**

T. J. was adopted when he was two years old. His racial makeup is white, black, and Japanese. His hometown is in the northeast region of Washington and western Idaho, and he is not always accepted. T. J. cannot stand idly by when an injustice occurs. His favorite teacher asks him to put together a swim team for his high school. T. J. selects the misfits of the school; this becomes a thorn in the side of the schools' jocks. They are determined that the swim team will not receive a letter in their sport. The team bonds and all benefit, but the price will be high for T.J. Soon he will realize how risky it is to be an adult.

Deuker, Carl. *High Heat.* **Houghton Mifflin, 2003. ISBN: 0-618-31117-3. Gr. 7-9**

Within six months it was all gone, the big house, Lexus cars, and private school education. Shane would never know whether his father was a criminal or not, but after he committed suicide, it did not matter. Now Shane waits at the public school bus stop with his head down while his former friends drive by. In his previous life, Shane was the closing pitcher at Shorelake; now he isn't sure if he even wants to play ball. Before long, Shane is in trouble with the police and part of his rehabilitation is to work on conditioning the local baseball field. He meets Coach Cornelius Grandison, who is also the coach at the public high school. Shane has a spot on the high school baseball team, but when he meets his former teammates in an unofficial game, his anger and resentment come out. Shane tricks the batter into stepping closer to the plate, then throws a fast ball on the inside. He hits Reese, the batter, who has to go to the hospital. Neither pitcher nor batter will ever be the same, and one year later they will meet in a playoff game.

Griffin, Adele. *Dive.* **Hyperion, 1999. ISBN: 0-7868-1567-1. Gr. 5-9**

Ben is 11 years old and chooses to live with his stable step-father. Half-brother Dustin has left his father and gone to live with the restless stepmother who is Ben's mother. When Dustin is in the hospital as a result of a diving accident, Ben and his stepfather rush to California to be at Dustin's side. Or was it an accident? Ben relays the story, confronts his mother, and realizes Dustin's self-destructive tendencies.

Gutman. Dan. *Jackie and Me: A Baseball Card Adventure.* **HarperCollins, 1999. ISBN: 0-380-97685-4. Gr. 3-7**

At school, Joe Stoshack is assigned a report on a famous African American who has made a contribution to society. Joe can use baseball cards to travel back in time, so he selects the Jackie Robinson card and travels back to the 1940s to get a first-hand impression of what it was like to be black and to break the color barrier in major league baseball.

Lynch, Chris. *Gold Dust.* **HarperCollins, 2002. ISBN: 0-06-447201-9. Gr. 5 & up**

The story takes place in 1975 in Boston when the Gold Dust Twins, Jim Rice and Fred Lynn, played for the Red Sox. Seventh-grader Richard Moncreif thinks only of baseball, until a new student from the Dominican Republic enrolls at his parochial school. Napoleon Ellis is black, upper middle class, well-spoken and plays cricket, and they become friends. Richard has a dream that the two of them will become the next Gold Dust Twins for the Red Sox. Unfortunately, Napoleon does not share that dream, and the racial tensions caused by the 1975 Boston bussing controversy eventually erode their friendship.

Scholastic Visual Sports Encyclopedia. **Scholastic Reference, 2003. ISBN: 0-439-31721-5. Juv**

This is an illustrated guide to more than 100 different sports. The chapters include "Track and Field," "Cycling," "Gymnastics," "Aquatic Sports," "Nautical Sports," "Equestrian Sports," "Precision and Accuracy," "Ice and Snow Sports," "Ball Sports," "Racket Sports," "Combat Sports," "Sports on Wheels," "Motor Sports," and "Multi Sports." Basic facts are included, such as, how each sport is played, what the rules are, what skills are needed, and what kind of equipment is used. A good overview with numerous illustrations and images of the playing fields, courts or courses associated with the sport. Nonfiction.

Skreslet, Laurie. *To the Top of Everest.* **Kids Can Press, 2001. ISBN: 1-55074-814-9. YA**

Laurie Shreslet was the first Canadian to climb Mount Everest. Without the help of his fellow climbers and the sherpas, Laurie would not have succeeded. This is the story of the entire expedition, from the packing of supplies by high school students, to the establishment of base camps, to the death of four members, to Laurie reaching the top of the world on October 5, 1982. He was the 131st person to climb the tallest mountain in the world. Nonfiction.

Wallace, Rich. *Losing Is Not an Option.* **Alfred A. Knopf, 2003. ISBN: 0-375-81351-9. Gr. 5-9**
>   Nine short stories about a young man and his interest in running, beginning in sixth-grade when he sneaks into the local high school football game for the 10th time by sprinting across an open lot. The thread of running is found in each short story and culminates in the final story with his life coming together personally and family-wise. He finds the strength and mental determination to win the state championship.

Zinnen, Linda. *Holding at Third.* **Dutton, 2004. ISBN: 0-525-47163-4. Gr. 5-8**
>   Matt is loyal to his cancer-stricken older brother, Tom, who must go to a neighboring city to receive a treatment of last resort. Matt leaves his school and home to support his mother and Tom. It is the beginning of baseball season when Matt starts at the new school and team. Matt seems to be okay on the surface, but when he goes into a batting slump, he begins to fall apart. Matt's ability to play baseball appears to be tied to Tom's struggle with his disease. With the help of his female coach, Matt learns to deal with his slump and Tom's disease.

Bibliography

Avi. *S.O.R. Losers.* Macmillan, 1984. ISBN: 0-02-793410-1. Gr. 5-7

Barwin, Steven, and Gabriel David Tick. *Slam Dunk.* Orca Paper, 1999. ISBN: 1-55028-598-X. Gr. 5-7

Bennett, James. *Blue Star Rapture.* Simon & Schuster, 1998. ISBN: 0-689-81580-8. Gr. 7-12

Bo, Ben. *The Edge.* Lerner, 1999. ISBN: 0-8225-3307-3. Gr. 5-8

———. *Skullcrack.* Lerner, 2000. ISBN: 0-8225-3307-3. Gr. 7-12

Brooks, Bruce. *Billy.* HarperCollins, 1998. ISBN: 0-06-027899-4. Gr. 4-8

———. *The Moves Make the Man.* Harper Trophy, 1996. ISBN: 0-06-440564-8. Gr. 7 & up

———. *Prince.* HarperCollins, 1998. ISBN: 0-06027542-1. Gr. 5-8

Bruchac, Joseph. *The Warriors.* Darby Creek, 2003. ISBN: 1-58196-002-6. Gr. 5-8

Butler, Kristin. *Cairo Kelly and the Man.* Orca Paper, 2002. ISBN: 1-55143-211-0. Gr. 4-8

Cadnum, Michael. *Redhanded.* Viking, 2000. ISBN: 0-670-88775-7. Gr. 8-10

Crutcher, Chris. *Ironman.* HarperCollins, 2004. ISBN: 0-06-059840-9. Juv

———. *Running Loose.* HarperCollins, 2003. ISBN: 0-06-009491-5. Juv

———. *Stotan!* HarperCollins, 2003. ISBN: 0-06-009492-3. Juv

Deans, Sis. *Racing the Past.* Henry Holt, 2001. ISBN: 0-8050-6635-7. Gr. 5-10

Deuker, Carl. *Night Hoops.* Houghton, 2000. ISBN: 0-395-97936-6. Gr. 7-11

Dygard, Thomas. *Running Wild.* Morrow/Avon, 1996. ISBN: 0-688-14853-0. Gr. 7 & up

———. *Second Stringer.* Morrow, 1998. ISBN: 0-688-15981-8. Gr. 6-12

Flynn, Pat. *Alex Jackson: SWA.* University of Queensland Paper, 2002. ISBN: 0-7022-3307-2. Gr. 6-10

Gallo, Donald R. *Ultimate Sports: Short Stories by Outstanding Writers for Young Adults.* Delacorte, 1995. ISBN: 0-385-31006-4. Juv

Griffis, Molly Levite. *The Great American Bunion Derby.* Eakin Press, 2003. ISBN: 1-57168-801-3. Gr. 4-6

Gutman, Dan. *Babe and Me.* Avon, 2000. ISBN: 0-380-97739-7. Gr. 5-7

———. *Honus and Me: A Baseball Card Adventure.* HarperTrophy, 1999. ISBN: 0-380-78878-0. Gr. 4-7

Hale, Daniel J. *Red Card.* Top Paper, 2002. ISBN: 1-929976-15-1. Gr. 4-7

Lipsyte, Robert. *The Brave.* HarperCollins Paper, 1991. ISBN: 0-06-447079-2. Gr. 8-12

———. *The Contender.* HarperCollins Paper, 1987. ISBN: 0-06-447039-3. Gr. 7 & up

———. *Warrior Angel.* HarperCollins, 2003. ISBN: 0-06-000496-7. Gr. 7-12

Lynch, Chris. *Shadow Boxer.* Harper Trophy, 1995. ISBN: 0-06-447112-8. Gr. 5 & up

Myers, Walter Dean. *Hoops.* Book Wholesalers, Inc., 2002. ISBN: 0-7587-4823-X. Juv

———. *The Journal of Biddy Owens.* Scholastic Paper, 2001. ISBN: 0-439-09503-4. Gr. 5-7

———. *Slam.* Scholastic Paper, 1996. ISBN: 0-590-48667-5. Gr. 8-12

Patneaude, David. *Haunting at Home Plate.* Albert Whitman, 2000. ISBN: 0-8075-3181-2. Gr. 4-7

Paulsen, Gary. *How Angel Peterson Got His Name and Other Outrageous Tales about Extreme Sports.* Random House, 2003. ISBN: 0-385-72949-9. Gr. 5 & up

Peers, Judi. *Shark Attack.* Orca Paper, 1999. ISBN: 1-55028-620-X. Gr. 5-7

Ritter, John H. *The Boy Who Saved Baseball.* Putnam, 2003. ISBN: 0-399-23622-8. Gr. 5-7

———. *Choosing Up Sides.* Putnam, 1998. ISBN: 0-399-23185-4. Gr. 5-9

———. *Over the Wall.* Putnam, 2000. ISBN: 0-399-23489-6. Gr. 6-10

Salisbury, Graham. *Lord of the Deep.* Random House, 2001. ISBN: 0-385-72918-9. Gr. 7 & up

Smith, Charles R. *Rimshots: Basketball Pix, Rolls, and Rhythms.* Dutton, 1999. ISBN: 0-525-46099-3. Gr. 5-9

———. *Tall Tales: Six Amazing Basketball Dreams.* Dutton, 2000. ISBN: 0-525-46172-8. Gr. 5-8

Trembath, Don. *Frog Face and the Three Boys.* Orca Paper, 2001. ISBN: 1-55143-165-3. Gr. 4-7

Wallace, Rich. *Playing Without the Ball: A Novel in Four Quarters.* Knopf, 2000. ISBN: 0-679-88672-9. Gr. 7-11

Weaver, Will. *Farm Team.* HarperCollins, 1999. ISBN: 0-06-447118-7. Juv

———. *Hard Ball.* HarperCollins, 1999. ISBN: 0-06-447208-6. Gr. 6 & up

———. *Striking Out.* HarperCollins, 1995. ISBN: 0-06-447113-6. Juv

Woolridge, Frosty. *Strike Three! Take Your Base.* Brookfield Reader, 2001. ISBN: 1-930093-01-2. Gr. 5-9

Zephaniah, Benjamin. *Face.* Bloomsbury, 2002. ISBN: 1-58234-774-3. Gr. 9-12

Zusak, Markus. *Fighting Ruben Wolfe.* Scholastic, 2001. ISBN: 0-439-24188-X. Gr. 8-12

Nonfiction

Aaseng, Nathan. *African-American Athletes.* Facts on File, 2003. ISBN: 0-8160-4805-3. Gr. 8-12

Bailey, John. *Fishing.* DK Paper, 2001. ISBN: 0-7894-7389-5. Gr. 5-8

Batten, Jack. *The Man Who Ran Faster Than Everyone: The Story of Tom Longboat.* Tundra Paper, 2002. ISBN: 0-88776-507-6. Gr. 7-12

Bernstein, Ross. *Kevin Garnett: Star Forward.* Enslow, 2002. ISBN: 0-7660-1829-6. Gr. 4-8

———. *Randy Moss: Star Wide Receiver.* Enslow, 2002. ISBN: 0-7660-1503-3. Gr. 4-8

Boards: The Art and Design of the Skateboard. Universe Publishing, 2003. ISBN: 0-7893-0977-7. Adult

Breton, Marcos. *Home Is Everything: The Latino Baseball Story.* Cinco Puntos Paper, 2003. ISBN: 0-938317-70-9. Gr. 7-12

Brooke, Michael. *The Concrete Wave: The History of Skateboarding.* Warwick, 1999. ISBN: 1-894020-54-5. Adult

Burgan, Michael. *Great Moments in Basketball.* World Almanac, 2002. ISBN: 0-8368-5345-8. Gr. 4-7

Ching, Jacqueline. *Adventure Racing.* Rosen, 2002. ISBN: 0-8239-3555-8. Gr. 7-10

Cole, Steve. *Kids' Easy Bike Care: Tune-Ups, Tools and Quick Fixes.* Williamson Paper, 2003. ISBN: 1-885593-86-4. Gr. 5-9

Cooper, John. *Rapid Ray: The Story of Ray Lewis.* Tundra Paper, 2002. ISBN: 0-88776-612-9. Gr. 5-9

Corbett, Doris, and John Cheffers, eds. *Unique Games and Sports around the World.* Greenwood, 2001. ISBN: 0-313-29778-9. Gr. 4-9

Crossingham, John. *Lacrosse in Action.* Crabtree, 2002. ISBN: 0-7787-0329-0. Gr. 4-7

———. *Cycling in Action.* Crabtree, 2002. ISBN: 0-7787-0118-2. Gr. 4-7

———. *Wrestling in Action.* Crabtree, 2003. ISBN: 0-7787-0336-3. Gr. 4-7

Crowther, Nicky. *The Ultimate Mountain Bike Book: The Definitive Illustrated Guide to Bikes, Components, Techniques, Thrills and Trails.* Firefly Paper, 2002. ISBN: 1-55297-653-X. Gr. 7-12

Curtis, Bruce, and Jay Morelli. *Beginning Golf.* Sterling, 2000. ISBN: 0-8069-4970-8. Gr. 5-8

DeAngelis, Gina. *Jackie Robinson: Overcoming Adversity.* Chelsea, 2000. ISBN: 0-7910-5897-2. Gr. 5-8

Dolan, Sean. *Michael Jordan: Basketball Great.* Chelsea House, 1994. ISBN: 0-7910-2151-3. Gr. 4-8

Dunning, Mark. *Basketball.* Sterling Paper, 2003. ISBN: 0-8069-9372-3. Gr. 4-8

Durant, Alan, selector. *Sports Stories.* Kingfisher, 2000. ISBN: 0-7534-5322-3. Gr. 5-9

Gedatus, Gus. *Weight Trainng.* Capstone, 2001. ISBN: 0-7368-0708-X. Gr. 4-7

Grabowski, John F. *The Boston Celtics.* Gale, 2003. ISBN: 1-56006-937-6. Gr. 7-9 (See others in series.)

Hayhurst, Chris. *Snowboarding! Shred the Powder.* Saddleback Publishing, 2000. ISBN: 1-56254-306-7. Gr. 5 & up

————. *Wakeboarding: Throw a Tantrum.* Rosen, 2000. ISBN: 0-8239-3008-4. Gr. 5-8

Howes, Chris. *Caving.* Heinemann, 2003. ISBN: 1-58810-626-8. Gr. 4-8

Johnstone, Mike. *NASCAR.* Lerner, 2002. ISBN: 0-8225-0389-1. Gr. 5-8

Kalman, Bobbie. *Bowling in Action.* Crabtree, 2003. ISBN: 0-7787-0335-5. Gr. 4-7

————. *Soccer in Action.* Sagebrush Education, 2000. ISBN: 0-613-22400-0. Gr. 3-6

Kaminsky, Marty. *Uncommon Champions: Fifteen Athletes Who Battled Back.* Boyds Mills, 2000. ISBN: 1-56397-787-7. Gr. 5-8

King, Daniel. *Chess: From First Moves to Checkmate.* Houghton, 2000. ISBN: 0-7534-5279-0. Gr. 4-6

Kingsbury, Robert. *Roberto Clemente.* Rosen, 2003. ISBN: 0-8239-3602-3. Gr. 4-7

Kneib, Martha. *Kareem Abdul-Jabbar.* Rosen, 2002. ISBN: 0-8239-3483-7. Gr. 5-8

Knotts, Bob. *Martial Arts.* Scholastic Paper, 2000. ISBN: 0-516-27028-1. Gr. 3-5

————. *Weightlifting.* Scholastic Paper, 2000. ISBN: 0-516-27032-X. Gr. 3-5

Krasner, Steven. *Play Ball Like the Pros: Tips for Kids from 20 Big League Stars.* Peachtree Paper, 2002. ISBN: 1-56145-261-0. Gr. 5-9

Lovitt, Chip. *Michael Jordan.* Scholastic Paper, 1998. ISBN: 0-590-59644-6. Gr. 6-10

Mason, Paul. *Skiing.* Heinemann, 2003. ISBN: 1-58810-628-4. Gr. 4-8

Mattern, Joanne. *Basketball Greats.* Gale, 2003. ISBN: 1-59018-228-6. Gr. 6-10

Miller, Calvin C. *Pete Sampras.* Morgan Reynolds, 1998. ISBN: 1-883846-26-9. Gr. 6-10

Myers, Walter Dean. *The Greatest: Muhammad Ali.* Scholastic Paper, 2001. ISBN: 0-590-54342-3. Gr. 6-10

O'Shei, Tim. *Mario Lemieux.* Chelsea, 2002. ISBN: 0-7910-6305-4. Gr. 8-12

Oxlade, Chris. *Rock Climbing.* Lerner, 2003. ISBN: 0-8225-1240-8. Gr. 3-6

Payan, Gregory. *Essential Snowmobiling for Teens.* Children's, 2000. ISBN: 0-516-23358-0. Gr. 5-9

Rekela, Jeff. *Brett Favre: Star Quarterback.* Enslow, 2000. ISBN: 0-7660-1332-4. Gr. 5-8

Ripkin, Cal, Jr., and Mike Bryan. *The Only Way I Know.* Penguin, 1998. ISBN: 0-14-026626-7. Adult

Roberts, Jeremy. *Rock and Ice Climbing!: Top the Tower.* Rosen, 2000. ISBN: 0-8239-3009-2. Gr. 5-8

Ryan, Pat. *Rock Climbing.* Smart Apple, 2000. ISBN: 1-887068-57-0. Gr. 4-7

Savage, Jeff. *Kobe Bryant: Basketball Big Shot.* Lerner, 2000. ISBN: 0-8225-3680-3. Gr. 4-7

———. *Top 10 Physically Challenged Athletes.* Enslow, 2000. ISBN: 0-7660-1272-7. Gr. 4-7

———. *Top 10 Sports Bloopers and Who Made Them.* Enslow, 2000. ISBN: 0-7660-1271-9. Gr. 4-7

Scheppler, Bill. *The Ironman Triathlon.* Rosen, 2002. ISBN: 0-8239-3556-6. Gr. 7-10

Schlegel, Elfi. *The Gymnastics Book: The Young Performer's Guide to Gymnastics.* Firefly Books, 2003. ISBN: 1-55209-414-6. Gr. 3-9

Schmidt, Julie. *Satchel Paige.* Rosen, 2002. ISBN: 0-8239-3478-0. Gr. 4-7

Spiros, Dean. *Top 10 Hockey Goalies.* Enslow, 1998. ISBN: 0-7660-1010-4. Gr. 6-9

Steenamer, Paul. *Mark Brunell: Star Quarterback.* Enslow, 2002. ISBN: 0-7660-1830-X. Gr. 4-8

Stewart, Mark. *Dale Earnhardt Jr.: Driven by Destiny.* Millbrook, 2003. ISBN: 0-7613-2908-0. Gr. 5-8

———. *Daunte Culpepper: Command and Control.* Millbrook, 2002. ISBN: 0-7613-2613-8. Gr. 4-7

———. *Ichiro Suzuki: Best in the West.* Millbrook, 2002. ISBN: 0-7613-2616-2. Gr. 4-7

———. *The Pettys: Triumphs and Tragedies of Auto Racing's First Family.* Millbrook, 2001. ISBN: 0-7613-2273-6. Gr. 4-8

———. *Sweet Victory: Lance Armstrong's Incredible Journey.* Millbrook, 2000. ISBN: 0-7613-1861-5. Gr. 6-10

———. *Tom Brady: Heart of the Huddle.* Millbrook, 2003. ISBN: 0-7613-2907-2. Gr. 4-7

Streissguth, Tom. *Jesse Owens.* Lerner, 1999. ISBN: 0-8225-4940-9. Gr. 6-12

Sullivan, George. *Baseball's Boneheads, Bad Boys, and Just Plain Crazy Guys.* Millbrook, 2003. ISBN: 0-7613-2321-X. Gr. 5-8

———. *Don't Step on the Foul Line: Sports Superstitions.* Millbrook, 2000. ISBN: 0-7613-1558-6. Gr. 4-8

Weekes, Don. *The Best and Worst of Hockey Firsts: The Unofficial Guide.* Douglas & McIntyre Paper, 2004. ISBN: 1-55-54-860-3. Adult

———. *Explosive Hockey Trivia: Puzzles, Games, Quizzes.* Douglas & McIntyre, 2004. ISBN: 1-55-054-851-4. Adult

Zeigler, Heidi. *Hang Gliding.* Scholastic, 2003. ISBN: 0-516-24320-9. Gr. 4-8

Picture Books

Golenbock, Peter. *Teammates.* Harcourt, 1990. ISBN: 0-15-200603-6. Juv

Kroeger, Mary Kay, and Louise Borden. *Paperboy.* Houghton Paper, 2001. ISBN: 0-618-11142-5. Juv

Leaf, Munro. *The Story of Ferdinand.* Penguin Group, 1936. ISBN: 0-670-67424-9. Juv

Paulsen, Gary. *Dogteam.* Random House, 1995. ISBN: 0-440-41130-0. Juv

Say, Allen. *Lost Lake.* Houghton Mifflin, 1989. ISBN: 0-395-50933-5. Juv

Shannon, David. *How Georgie Radbourn Saved Baseball.* Scholastic, 1994. ISBN: 0-590-47410-3. Juv

Annotated Journal Article

Myers, Walter Dean. "Pulling No Punches: Edwards Award Winner Robert Lipsyte Talks to Walter Dean Myers." *School Library Journal* **(June 2001):44-47.**

Walter Dean Myers discusses with Robert Lipsyte how difficult it is to get kids to read today and the issues that kids are dealing with. Lipsyte shares stories of his childhood and tells how his experiences gave him ideas for his books. Lipsyte writes about sports and manhood and talks about writing for today's youth.

7

War

Introduction

Many boys are happiest when they are in some sort of pretend military combat. They see more than enough fighting in the news, on the television, in the movies, and in video games. So it is logical that they would be interested in war diaries and books about the armed forces, special forces, military jets, aircraft carriers, and submarines. Stories that tell of life in times of war and books that describe wars of the past are of interest.

Discussion Questions

- Do you know of anyone in the military?

- How did you become interested in this topic?

- Did this book enhance your knowledge of this topic?

- Were the illustrations/photos well done?

- Did they help you to have a better understanding of the text?

Annotations

Bearden, Romare. *Li'L Dan the Drummer Boy: A Civil War Story.* **Simon & Schuster Books for Young Readers, 2003. ISBN: 0-689-86237-7. Juv**

Li'l Dan was written and illustrated by this famous African-American artist over two decades ago. It is the story of a young slave boy who learns how to play the drum from a fellow slave. When the Union soldiers come to his plantation and tell all the slaves that they are free, Li'l Dan is confused and has nowhere to go. The soldiers feed Li'l Dan, so he follows them. He becomes the mascot of Company E and the soldiers enjoy listening to him play his drum in the evening. One night, Company E is called to march and no one notices that Li'l Dan is along. When they realize he is there they tell him to go back and wait until they come for him. Li'l Dan climbs a tree and sees that his friends are about to be ambushed by the Confederates. Li'l Dan remembers the sound of cannon fire, and warns Company E by duplicating the sound on his drum. Maya Angelou narrates *Li'l Dan the Drummer Boy* on the accompanying CD. Picture book.

Clinton, Catryn. *A Stone in My Hand.* **Candlewick Press, 2002. ISBN: 0-7636-1388-6. Gr. 5-12**

Malaak's father, a Palestinian, was missing and presumed dead when the bus he was riding on was blown up by the Islamic Jihad. Now Hamid, her brother, is hanging around religious zealots and Malaak is afraid that he will join the radical group. His mother confronts Hamid and tells him that he will never be a member of the Islamic Jihad. Hamid agrees but is gravely wounded when he is shot by an Israeli soldier for throwing stones. The story is told from Malaak's point of view; when her father disappears and Hamid is shot, she retreats to her quiet place and cannot speak. Now Hamid is in a coma and needs Malaak to be brave, understanding of the Palestinian cause, and by his side.

Damon, Duane. *Growing Up in the Civil War, 1861 to 1865.* **Lerner Publishing, 2002. ISBN: 0-8225-0656-4. Juv**

Primary documents, such as letters, diaries, newspapers, songs, paintings, and photographs, are used "to see how young people lived, talked, and thought during the Civil War period." The author intersperses quotes and stories from a cross-section of males, females, Northern, Southern, city, country, rich, poor, free, and slave. Nonfiction.

Hughes, Dean. *Soldier Boys.* **Simon Pulse, 2001. ISBN: 0-689-81748-7. Gr. 4-6**

A close-up view of war is presented from the opposing perspectives of two young boys. Spencer, from Utah, is 17 years old, and Dieter is a leader in Hitler's Youth section. Both are idealistic and anxious to enter the war before it ends. Eventually they meet on an open hill near some forests in Belgium. Both change on that hill, and neither one will want to continue fighting. Only one will survive, and the remaining one will think about that day the rest of his life.

Murray, Aaron R., ed. *Civil War Battles and Leaders.* **DK Paper, 2004. ISBN: 0-7894-9891-X. Juv**

More than 200 photographs, portraits, artifacts, and maps illustrate this chronology of the Civil War. The book is divided as follows: "1861: First Clashes on the Road to War," "1862: The War in the South Intensifies," "1863: High Tide for the Confederacy," "1864: Total War in the Confederacy," and "1865: Grant Traps Lee, Pursuit to Appomattox." Nonfiction.

Myers, Walter Dean. *Patrol: An American Soldier in Vietnam.* HarperCollins Publishers, 2002. ISBN: 0-06-028364-5. Gr. 3-7

A young soldier is in the forests of Vietnam, when he comes in contact with the enemy. They stare at each other across the field, each not willing to raise their rifles. A helicopter breaks up the moment; the young soldier is taken out of harm's way and lands safely to fight another day. Picture book.

Orlev, Uri. *Run, Boy, Run.* Houghton Mifflin, 2003. ISBN: 0-618-16465-0. Gr. 5 & up

After years of denying he is a Jew, Jurek Staniak will forget his real name, the names of his parents, brothers, and sisters. However, he does not forget the hastily spoken words of his father minutes before he sacrificed his life to save eight-year-old Jurek. His father tells him to find someone to teach him how to act like a Christian and to find a farmer to stay with until the war is over. He tells him to run to the forest and find water or swamps if followed by dogs. Jurek follows his father's advice and uses his winning personality and undaunted courage to escape starvation, Polish winters, and capture by the Germans.

Philip, Neil. *War and the Pity of War.* Houghton Mifflin, 1998. ISBN: 0-395-84982-9. Gr. 5-9

Poetry about all aspects of war from ancient Greece to the 20th century. The soldier's experiences are similar no matter the time period. The horrors of war as well as the bravery and courage of both the soldiers and civilians are depicted. Nonfiction.

Rappaport, Doreen, and Joan Verniero. *Victory or Death! Stories of the American Revolution.* HarperCollins, 2003. ISBN: 0-06-029515-5. Juv

There were many heroes of the American Revolution; these stories feature men and women, many who are not well known. Sybil Ludington, 16 years old, rode 40 miles all night to muster her father's' troops, who were on leave, to stop British soldiers 12 miles away. Francis Salvador visited the back country of South Carolina to "win converts to the cause of independence and to get them to swear an oath of loyalty." Other stories about heroes include Peter Brown, Abigail Adams, George Washington, Grace Growden Galloway, James Armistead, and Robert Shurtliff. Includes books and Web sites for young readers.

Bibliography

Adler, Elizabeth. *Crossing the Panther's Path.* Farrar, Straus & Giroux, 2002. ISBN: 0-374-31662-7. Gr. 6-8

Armstrong, Jennifer, ed. *Shattered: Stories of Children and War.* Knopf, 2002. ISBN: 0-385-81112-5. Gr. 6-9

Ashley, Bernard. *Little Soldier.* Scholastic, 2002. ISBN: 0-439-22424-1. Gr. 7-10

Avi. *Don't You Know There's a War On?* HarperCollins, 2001. ISBN: 0-06-029214-8. Gr. 4-7

Bagdasarian, Adam. *Forgotten Fire.* DK Paper, 2000. ISBN: 0-7894-2627-7. Gr. 8-12

Beach, Edward L. *Run Silent, Run Deep.* Naval Institute Press, 1986. ISBN: 0-87021-557-4. Adult

Brown, Don. *Our Time on the River.* Houghton, 2003. ISBN: 0-618-31116-5. Gr. 7-10

Cadnum, Michael. *The Book of the Lion.* Viking, 2000. ISBN: 0-670-88386-7. Gr. 7-12

Choi, Sook Nyul. *Year of Impossible Goodbyes.* Houghton, 1991. ISBN: 0-395-57419-6. Gr. 6-9

Crisp, Marty. *Private Captain: A Story of Gettysburg.* Philomel, 2001. ISBN: 0-399-23577-9. Gr. 6-8

Crist-Evans, Craig. *Amaryllis.* Candlewick Press, 2003. ISBN: 0-7836-1863-2. Gr. 10-12

———. *Moon Over Tennessee: A Boy's Civil War Journal.* Houghton Mifflin, 1999. ISBN: 0-395-91208-3. Gr. 4-7

Denenberg, Barry. *The Journal of William Thomas Emerson: A Revolutionary War Patriot.* Scholastic Paper, 1998. ISBN: 0-590-31350-9. Gr. 4-8

Elliot, L. M. *Under a War-Torn Sky.* Hyperion, 2003. ISBN: 0-7868-1753-4. Gr. 6-9

Ellis, Deborah. *Parvana's Journey.* Groundwood, 2004. ISBN: 0-88899-51-8. Gr. 5-9

Ernst, Kathleen. *Ghosts of Vicksburg.* White Mane, 2003. ISBN: 1-57249322-4. Gr. 6-10

———. *Retreat from Gettysburg.* White Mane, 2000. ISBN: 1-57249-187-6. Gr. 5-8

Fox, Carol, et al. *In Times of War: An Anthology of War and Peace in Children's Literature.* Pavilion, 2001. ISBN: 1-86205-446-0. Gr. 6-12

Gaeddert, Lou Ann. *Friends and Enemies.* Simon & Schuster, 2000. ISBN: 0-689-82822-5. Gr. 6-9

Garland, Sherry. *In the Shadow of the Alamo.* Harcourt, 2001. ISBN: 0-15-201744-5. Gr. 5-8

Griffis, Molly Levite. *The Feester Filibuster.* Eakin, 2002. ISBN: 1-57168-541-3. Gr. 4-8

Hahn, Mary Downing. *Hear the Wind Blow: A Novel of the Civil War.* Clarion, 2003. ISBN: 0-618-18190-3. Gr. 6-9

Havill, Juanita. *Eyes Like Willy's.* HarperCollins, 2004. ISBN: 0-688-13672-9. Gr. 6-9

Hesse, Karen. *Aleutian Sparrow.* Simon & Schuster, 2003. ISBN: 0-689-86189-3. Gr. 5-10

Hite, Sid. *The Journal of Rufus Rowe: A Witness to the Battle of Fredericksburg.* Scholastic, 2003. ISBN: 0-439-35364-5. Gr. 5-7

Ho, Minfong. *Gathering the Dew.* Orchard, 2003. ISBN: 0-439-38197-5. Gr. 6-9

Hughes, Pat. *Guerilla Season.* Farrar, Straus & Giroux, 2003. ISBN: 0-374-32811-0. Gr. 7-12

Kimmel, Eric A. *Sword of the Samurai: Adventure Stories from Japan.* Harcourt, 1999. ISBN: 0-15-201985-5. Gr. 4-8

Lawrence, Iain. *Lord of the Nutcracker Men.* Delacorte, 2001. ISBN: 0-385-72924-3. Gr. 5-9

Lisle, Janet T. *The Art of Keeping Cool.* Simon & Schuster, 2000. ISBN: 0-689-83787-9. Gr. 5-8

Lowry, Lois. *Number the Stars.* Houghton, 1989. ISBN: 0-395-51060-0. Gr. 4-8

Mazer, Harry. *A Boy at War: A Novel of Pearl Harbor.* Simon & Schuster, 2001. ISBN: 0-689-84161-2. Gr. 7-9

———. *The Last Mission.* Dell, 1981. ISBN: 0-440-94797-9. Gr. 7 & up

Myers, Walter Dean. *Fallen Angels.* Scholastic, 2003. ISBN: 0-590-40943-3. Gr. 7 & up

———. *The Journal of Scott Pendleton Collins: A World War II Soldier.* Scholastic, 1999. ISBN: 0-439-05013-8. Gr. 5-9

Napoli, Donna Jo. *Stones in Water.* Puffin, 1997. ISBN: 0-14-130600-9. Gr. 5-9

Orlev, Uri. *The Island on Bird Street.* Houghton, 1984. ISBN: 0-395-33887-5. Gr. 5-9

Park, Linda Sue. *When My Name Was Keoko.* Clarion, 2002. ISBN: 0-618-13335-6. Gr. 5-9

Paulsen, Gary. *Soldier's Heart: Being the Story of the Enlistment and Due Service of the Boy Charley Goddard in the First Minnesota Volunteers.* Random House, 2000. ISBN: 0-440-22838-7. Gr. 7-12

Peck, Richard. *The River between Us.* Dial Books for Young Readers, 2003. ISBN: 0-8037-2735-6. Gr. 5-10

Propp, Vera W. *When the Soldiers Were Gone.* Putnam, 1999. ISBN: 0-399-23325-3. Gr. 4-9

Reeder, Carolyn. *Before the Creeks Ran Red.* HarperCollins, 2003. ISBN: 0-06-623615-0. Gr. 6-9

Richardson, George C. *Drummer.* Writer's Showcase Paper, 2001. ISBN: 0-595-15359-3. Gr. 6-9

Ross, Stewart. *The Star Houses: A Story from the Holocaust.* Barron's, 2002. ISBN: 0-7641-5528-8. Gr. 4-8

Satrapi, Marjane. *Persepolis: The Story of a Childhood.* Knopf, 2003. ISBN: 0-375-42230-7. Adult

Shaara, Michael. *The Killer Angels.* Ballantine, 1996. ISBN: 0-345-40727-X. Adult

Spinelli, Jerry. *Milkweed.* Knopf, 2003. ISBN: 0-375-81374-8. Gr. 7 & up

Tunnell, Michael O. *Brothers in Valor: A Story of Resistance.* Holiday House, 2001. ISBN: 0-8234-1541-4. Gr. 6-10

Watkins, Yoko Kawashima. *So Far from the Bamboo Grove.* HarperTempest, 1986. ISBN: 0-688-13115-8. Gr. 6-10

Whelan, Gloria. *Angel on the Square.* HarperCollins, 2001. ISBN: 0-06-029030-7. Gr. 5 & up

White, Ellen Emerson. *The Journal of Patrick Seamus Flaherty: United States Marine Corps.* Scholastic, 2002. ISBN: 0-439-14890-1. Gr. 6-9

Wilson, John. *And in the Morning.* Kids Can Press, 2003. ISBN: 1-55337-400-2. Gr. 8-12

Wisler, G. Clifton. *Kings Mountain.* HarperCollins, 2002. ISBN: 0-06-623793-9. Gr. 5-7

———. *Run the Blockade.* HarperCollins, 2000. ISBN: 0-06-029208-3. Gr. 5-8

Wulffson, Don. *Soldier X.* Viking, 2001. ISBN: 0-670-88863-X. Gr. 8-12

Zindel, Paul. *The Gadget.* HarperCollins, 2001. ISBN: 0-06-027812-9. Gr. 6-12

Nonfiction

Aaseng, Nathan. *Navajo Code Talkers.* Walker, 1992. ISBN: 0-8027-8183-7. Gr. 6-9

Abells, Chana Byers. *The Children We Remember.* Greenwillow, 1986. ISBN: 0-688-06371-3. Gr. 2-8

al-Windawi, Thura. *Thura's Diary: My Life in Wartime Iraq.* Viking, 2004. ISBN: 0-670-05886-6. Gr. 7-12

Allen, Thomas B. *Remember Pearl Harbor: American and Japanese Survivors Tell Their Stories.* National Geographic, 2001. ISBN: 0-7922-6690-0. Gr. 5-9

Altman, Linda Jacobs. *The Forgotten Victims of the Holocaust.* Enslow, 2003. ISBN: 0-7660-1993-4. Gr. 5-10

Amis, Nancy. *The Orphans of Normandy: A True Story of World War II Told through Drawings by Children.* Simon & Schuster, 2003. ISBN: 0-689-84143-4. Gr. 2-8

Anderson, Paul Christopher. *Robert E. Lee: Legendary Commander of the Confederacy.* Rosen, 2003. ISBN: 0-8239-5748-9. Gr. 4-7

Anflick, Charles. *Teen Partisan and Resisters Who Fought Nazi Tyranny.* Rosen, 1999. ISBN: 0-8239-2847-0. Gr. 5-9

Axelrod, Toby. *Rescuers Defying the Nazis: Non-Jewish Teens Who Rescued Jews.* Rosen, 1999. ISBN: 0-8239-2848-9. Gr. 5-8

Bolotin, Norman. *Civil War A to Z: A Young Person's Guide to Over 100 People, Places, and Points of Importance.* Dutton, 2002. ISBN: 0-525-46268-6. Gr. 4-8

Brubaker, Paul. *The Cuban Missile Crisis in American History.* Enslow, 2001. ISBN: 0-7660-1414-2. Gr. 6-10

Bruning, John Robert. *Elusive Glory: African-American Heroes of World War II.* Avisson Paper, 2001. ISBN: 1-888105-48-8. Gr. 5-8

Burch, Joann. *Jefferson Davis: President of the Confederacy.* Enslow, 1998. ISBN: 0-7660-1064-3. Gr. 5-8

Cameron, Sara. *Out of War: True Stories from the Front Lines of the Children's Movement for Peace in Colombia.* Scholastic, 2001. ISBN: 0-439-29721-4. Gr. 5-10

Cooper, Michael L. *Remembering Manzanar: Life in a Japanese Relocation Camp.* Clarion, 2002. ISBN: 0-618-06778-7. Gr. 4-9

Dennenberg, Barry. *Voices from Vietnam.* Scholastic, 1995. ISBN: 0-590-44267-8. Gr. 7-12

Drucker, Olga Levy. *Kindertransport.* Holt, 2002. ISBN: 0-8050-4251-2. Gr. 5-10

Ferrie, Richard. *The World Turned Upside Down: George Washington and the Battle of Yorktown.* Holiday, 1999. ISBN: 0-8234-1402-7. Gr. 5-8

Fradin, Dennis. *Samuel Adams: The Father of American Independence.* Clarion, 1998. ISBN: 0-395-82510-5. Gr. 4-6

———. *Who Was Ben Franklin?* Holiday, 2002. ISBN: 0-448-42495-9. Gr. 3-5

Freedman, Russell. *Give Me Liberty! The Story of the Declaration of Independence.* Holiday, 2000. ISBN: 9-8234-1448-5. Gr. 4-7

Fritz, Jean. *Why Not, Lafayette?* Putnam, 1999. ISBN: 0-399-23411-X. Gr. 4-7

Gaines, Ann Graham. *Douglas MacArthur: Brilliant General Controversial Leader.* Enslow, 2001. ISBN: 0-7660-1445-2. Gr. 5-8

Gay, Kathlyn, and Martin Gay. *Korean War.* Twenty-First Century, 1996. ISBN: 0-8050-4100-1. Gr. 6-8

———. *Persian Gulf War.* Twenty-First Century, 1996. ISBN: 0-8050-4102-8. Gr. 6-8

———. *Vietnam War.* Twenty-First Century, 1996. ISBN: 0-8050-4101-X. Gr. 6-8

Gonzales, Doreen. *The Manhattan Project and the Atomic Bomb in American History.* Enslow, 2000. ISBN: 0-98490-879-0. Gr. 6-12

Grant, R. G. *Hiroshima and Nagasaki.* Raintree Steck-Vaughn, 1998. ISBN: 0-8172-5013-1. Gr. 7-12

Green, Carl R., and William R. Sanford. *Confederate Generals of the Civil War.* Enslow, 1998. ISBN: 0-7660-1029-5. Gr. 5-8

———. *Union Generals of the Civil War.* Enslow, 1998. ISBN: 0-7660-1028-7. Gr. 5-8

Holden, Henry M. *The Persian Gulf War.* Enslow, 2003. ISBN: 0-7660-5109-9. Gr. 4-8

Hook, Jason. *Hiroshima August 6, 1945.* Raintree Steck-Vaughn, 2003. ISBN: 0-7398-5234-5. Gr. 6-8

Keeley, Jennifer. *Life in the Hitler Youth.* Lucent, 1999. ISBN: 1-56006-613-X. Gr. 7-12

Kent, Zachary. *The Persian Gulf War: "The Mother of All Battles."* Enslow, 1994. ISBN: 0-89490-528-7. Gr. 5-7

Knapp, Ron. *American Generals of World War II.* Enslow, 1998. ISBN: 0-7660-1024-4. Gr. 5-8

Kort, Michael G. *The Handbook of the Middle East.* Twenty-First Century, 2002. ISBN: 0-7613-1611-6. Gr. 7-12

Levine, Ellen. *Darkness over Denmark: The Danish Resistance and the Rescue of the Jews.* Holiday, 2000. ISBN: 0-8234-1447-7. Gr. 6-12

Levine, Karen. *Hana's Suitcase.* Albert Whitman, 2003. ISBN: 0-8075-3148-0. Gr. 5-8

Lobel, Anita. *No Pretty Pictures: A Child of War.* Greenwillow Books, 1998. ISBN: 0-688-15935-4. Gr. 5 & up

Longfellow, Henry Wadsworth. *The Midnight Ride of Paul Revere.* Handprint, 2001. ISBN: 1-929766-13-0. Gr. 3-7

Marrin, Albert. *Commander in Chief Abraham Lincoln and the Civil War.* Dutton, 1997. ISBN: 0-525-45822-0. Gr. 7-12

Marshood, Nabil. *Palestinian Teenage Refugees and Immigrants Speak Out.* Rosen, 1997. ISBN: 0-8239-2442-4. Gr. 7-12

McKain, Mark, ed. *Making and Using the Atomic Bomb.* Gale, 2003. ISBN: 0-7377-1412-3. Gr. 8-12

McKissack, Patricia C., and Frederick L. McKissack. *Days of Jubilee: The End of Slavery in the United States.* Scholastic, 2003. ISBN: 0-590-10764-X. Gr. 4-8

McPherson, James M. *Field of Fury: The American Civil War.* Simon & Schuster, 2002. ISBN: 0-689-84833-1. Gr. 6-8

Panchyk, Richard. *World War II for Kids: A History with 21 Activities.* Chicago Review Paper, 2002. ISBN: 1-55652-455-2. Gr. 5-7

Rice, Earle. *The Nuremberg Trials.* Lucent, 1996. ISBN: 1-56006-269-X. Gr. 6-10

————. *The Tet Offensive.* Lucent, 1996. ISBN: 1-56006-422-6. Gr. 6-10 (See others in this series.)

Roberts, Russell. *Leaders and Generals (Vietnam).* Lucent, 2001. ISBN: 1-56006-717-9. Gr. 6-12

Rogow, Sally M. *Faces of Courage: Young Heroes of World War II.* Granville Island, 2003. ISBN: 1-89494-20-1. Gr. 5-9

Rubin, Susan Goldman. *Fireflies in the Dark: The Story of Friedl Dicker-Brandeis and the Children of Terezin.* Holiday, 2000. ISBN: 0-8234-1461-2. Gr. 4 & up

Saenger, Diana, and Bradley Steffens. *Life as a POW.* Lucent, 2001. ISBN: 1-56006-716-0. Gr. 6-12

Shaffer, David. *The Iran-Iraq War.* Gale, 2002. ISBN: 1-59018-184-0. Gr. 5-8

Silverman, Jerry. *Songs and Stories of the Civil War.* Twenty-First Century, 2002. ISBN: 0-7613-2305-8. Gr. 6-9

Tanaka, Sheila. *A Day That Changed America: Gettysburg.* Hyperion, 2003. ISBN: 0-7868-1922-7. Gr. 3 & up

Tryszynska-Frederick, Luba, and Michelle R. McCann. *Luba: The Angel of Bergen-Belsen.* Tricycle, 2003. ISBN: 1-58246-098-1. Gr. 3-7

Tunnell, Michael O., and George W. Chilcoat. *The Children of Topaz: The Story of a Japanese-American Internment Camp, Based on a Classroom Diary.* Holiday, 1996. ISBN: 0-8234-1239-3. Gr. 3-8

Wagner, Heather Lehr. *Israel and the Arab World.* Chelsea, 2002. ISBN: 0-7910-6705-X. Gr. 6-12

Warren, Andrea. *Surviving Hitler: A Boy in the Nazi Death Camps.* HarperCollins, 2001. ISBN: 0-688-17497-3. Gr. 5-10

White, Matt. *Cameras on the Battlefield: Photos of War.* Capstone, 2002. ISBN: 0-7368-4004-4. Gr. 5-7

Whitelaw, Nancy. *The Shot Heard Around the World: The Battles of Lexington and Concord.* Morgan Reynolds, 2001. ISBN: 1-883846-75-7. Gr. 5-8

Wisler, G. Clifton. *When Johnny Went Marching: Young Americans Fight the Civil War.* HarperCollins, 2001. ISBN: 0-688-16537-0. Gr. 5-8

Picture Books

Balgassi, Haemi. *Peacebound Trains.* Clarion, 1996. ISBN: 0-395-72093-1. Juv

Bunting, Eve. *So Far from the Sea.* Houghton Mifflin, 1998. 0-395-72095-8. Juv

———. *The Wall.* Clarion Books, 1990. ISBN: 0-618-44297-9. Juv

Craddock, Sonia. *Sleeping Boy.* Simon & Schuster, 1999. ISBN: 0-689-81763-0. Juv

Deedy, Carmen Agra. *The Yellow Star: The Legend of King Christian X of Denmark.* Peachtree, 2000. ISBN: 1-56145-208-4. Juv

Gauch, Particia Lee. *Thunder at Gettysburg.* Boyds Mills Press, 2003. ISBN: 1-59078-180-5. Juv

Granfield, Linda. *In Flanders Field: The Story of the Poem by John McCrae.* Stoddart Kids, 2000. ISBN: 0-7737-5925-5. Juv

Heide, Florence Parry, and Judith Heide Gilliland. *Sami and the Time of the Troubles.* Clarion, 1992. ISBN: 0-395-55964-2. Juv

Hoffman, Mary. *The Color of Home.* Penguin Putnam, 2002. ISBN: 0-8037-2841-7. Juv

Innocenti, Roberto. *Rose Blanche.* Creative, 1995. ISBN: 1-568-46189-5. Juv

Keller, Holly. *Grandfather's Dream.* Greenwillow Books, 1994. ISBN: 0-688-12339-2. Juv

Lyon, George Ella. *Cecil's Story.* Orchard, 1995. ISBN: 0-531-07063-8. Juv

Maruki, Toshi. *Hiroshima No Pika.* HarperCollins, 1982. ISBN: 0-688-01297-3. Juv

Mochizuki, Ken. *Baseball Saved Us.* Lee & Low, 1993. ISBN: 1-880000-01-6. Juv

———. *Passage to Freedom: The Sugihara Story.* Lee & Low, 1997. ISBN: 1-880000-49-0. Juv

Park, Frances, and Ginger Park. *My Freedom Trip: A Child's Escape from North Korea.* Boyds Mills, 2003. ISBN: 1-56397-468-1. Juv

Polacco, Patricia. *The Butterfly.* Philomel, 2000. ISBN: 0-399-23170-6. Juv

———. *Pink and Say.* Scholastic, 1998. ISBN: 0-439-04467-7. Juv

Say, Allen. *Home of the Brave.* Houghton/Walter Lorraine, 2002. ISBN: 0-618-21223-X. Juv

Seuss, Dr. *The Butter Battle Book.* Random, 1984. ISBN: 0-394-86580-4. Juv

Tsuchiya, Yukio. *Faithful Elephants: A True Story of Animals, People, and War.* Houghton Mifflin, 1988. ISBN: 0-395-46555-9. Juv

Annotated Journal Article

Farish, Terry. "Children of War." *School Library Journal* **(January 2004): 38-39.**
    The author shares some startling facts about the casualties of contemporary war that are found in daily newspapers. These same facts are so much more poignant and haunting when they are shared in a novel written through the eyes of the children who are involved in these conflicts. The article reviews these novels.

8

Biography

Introduction

Boys like to read about the lives of famous people. These can be sports professionals or inventors or actors and actresses. They like to find out where these people came from and how they got to be considered famous. They like to compare their lives and imagine what it would be like to be famous. They like to strive to be like these people.

Discussion Questions

- Had you known about this person before reading this book?

- Did this book clarify misunderstandings you might have had about this person?

- Will you read other accounts of this person's life?

- How do you think the author got all the information to write this book?

- Do you think everything in this book is true?

- Do you know anyone like this person?

- Do you read other biographies of this type?

Annotations

Demi. *Gandhi.* **Margaret K. McElderry Books, 2001. ISBN: 0-689-84149-3. Juv**

Gandhi was a shy man who married according to custom at the age of 13. He went to London and studied law. He experienced racism when in 1893 he went to work in South Africa. He created the theory of satyagraha, or the force of selfless love, which advocates love and peace to overcome violence. Gandhi returned to India in 1915 and worked to rid India of its caste system and British oppression. Picture book.

Fleming, Candace. *Ben Franklin's Almanac: Being a True Account of the Good Gentleman's Life.* **Atheneum Books for Young Readers, 2003. ISBN: 0-689-83549-3. Gr. 5-9**

This account of Ben Franklin's life is done as a scrapbook with portraits, etchings, cartoons, and sketches. The gathered information is arranged by subject in chapters: "Boyhood Memories," "The Family Album," "The Writer's Journal," "Tokens of a Well-Lived Life," "The Scientist's Scrapbook," "Revolutionary Memorabilia," "Souvenirs from France," and "Final Remembrances." One can read a selection from any chapter and in any order find out something interesting about Ben; for example, in "Tokens of a Well-Lived Lived Life," Ben asked himself every morning, what good shall I do today? and at the end of the day, what good had I done that day?

Gantos, Jack. *Hole in My Life.* **Farrar, Straus & Giroux, 2002. ISBN: 0-374-39988-3. YA**

While locked up in prison, Jack Gantos realizes that he must make better decisions and stop thinking about being a writer. During his last years of high school, Jack is adrift, living on his own, and smoking pot. In time, Jack joins his family in St. Croix, becomes part of the drug culture, and helps sail a boat loaded with 2,000 pounds of hash up to New York. Trouble follows and Jack is wanted by the FBI. One of the crew members has been in contact with the FBI from the beginning. Photos are taken of the whole operation, and Jack is sentenced to six months to five years in prison. During his 15 months in prison, Jack settles down and concentrates on his writing and plans for the future.

Mochizuki, Ken. *Passage to Freedom: The Sugihara Story.* **Lee & Low Books, 1997. ISBN: 1-880000-49-0. Gr. 1-6**

Passage to Freedom is told from the son's point of view. It is about his father, who is a diplomat from Japan in Poland just before World War II. One morning, a crowd of Jews from Poland line up in front of their house asking for visas to go to Japan. The boy's father disobeys his superiors and issues visas by hand to the Polish Jews for one month until he is forced to leave his home because of the approaching Russians and Germans.

Robinson, Sharon. *Promises to Keep: How Jackie Robinson Changed America.* **Scholastic Press, 2004. ISBN: 0-439-42592-1. Juv**

This photo-biography of Jackie Robinson delineates his commitment to America and his challenge to all of us. Jackie Robinson helped break down racial segregation by being the first black man to play in the Major Baseball League. After a successful career in baseball, he retired in 1956 at 37 years of age. In 1962, he was elected to the Baseball Hall of Fame. Jackie Robinson continued his commitment to America and received the nation's highest civilian award, the Presidential Medal of Freedom. In 1972, after he died, the Jackie Robinson Foundation was established to provide education and leadership development opportunities to young people with the expectation that they will give back to their communities. Jackie lived his philosophy: "A life is not important except for the impact it has on other lives."

Sis, Peter. *Starry Messenger.* **Farrar, Straus & Giroux, 1996. ISBN: 0-374-37191-1. Juv**

Galileo makes a telescope for himself, after hearing about how one is made. He writes his observations in a book entitled *The Starry Messenger.* His observations become popular, and the Church worries that his idea, that the earth is not the center of the universe, has gone against the Bible. Galileo is tried and punished. He is to spend the rest of his life locked in his house. The fact that he is locked up does not stop Galileo from continuing his work and passing along his ideas. Picture book.

Stanley, Diane. *Saladin: Noble Prince of Islam.* **HarperCollins Publishers, 2002. ISBN: 0-688-17135-4. Gr. 5-8**

Just before he died in 1193, Saladin gave his eldest son advice on being a king: "Win the hearts of your people and watch over their prosperity; for it is to secure their happiness that you are appointed by God and by me." Saladin was a gentle Muslim warrior who shocked his enemy with his mercy when victorious. He was a warrior who longed for peace and was considered a "marvel of his time."

Bibliography

Anderson, Robert. *Salvador Dali.* Watts, 2002. ISBN: 0-531-16624-4. Gr. 5-8

Bankston, John. *Diego Rivera.* Mitchell Lane, 2003. ISBN: 1-58415-208-7. Gr. 5-7

———. *Juan Bautista de Anza.* Mitchell Lane, 2003. ISBN: 1-58415-196-X. Gr. 5-7

Blashfield, Jean F. *Leonard Bernstein: Composer and Conductor.* Ferguson, 2001. ISBN: 0-89434-337-8. Gr. 4-7

Bolton, Linda. *Andy Warhol.* Watts, 2002. ISBN: 0-531-12225-5. Gr. 5-8

Brown, Gene. *Duke Ellington: Jazz Master.* Blackbirch, 2001. ISBN: 1-56711-505-5. Gr. 7-10

Burgan, Michael. *Franklin D. Roosevelt.* Compass Point, 2002. ISBN: 0-7565-0203-9. Gr. 4-8

Burnett, Betty. *Ferdinand Magellan: The First Voyage Around the World.* Rosen, 2003. ISBN: 0-8239-3617-1 Gr. 4-7

Byrd, Robert. *Leonardo: Beautiful Dreamer.* Dutton, 2002. ISBN: 0-525-47033-6. Gr. 3-8

Calvert, Patricia. *Robert E. Peary: To the Top of the World.* Marshall Cavendish, 2001. ISBN: 0-7614-1242-5. Gr. 5-8

Cooper, Ilene. *Jack: The Early Years of John F. Kennedy.* Dutton, 2003. ISBN: 0-525-46923-0. Gr. 7-12

Crutcher, Chris. *King of the Mild Frontier: An Ill-Advised Autobiography.* Greenwillow Books, 2003. ISBN: 0-06-050249-5. Gr. 8-12

Currie, Stephen. *Polar Explorers.* Gale, 2002. ISBN: 1-56006-957-0. Gr. 5-9

Demi. *Muhammad.* Simon & Schuster, 2003. ISBN: 0-689-85264-9. Gr. 3-7

Draper, Allison Stark. *Vasco da Gama: The Portuguese Quest for a Sea Route from Europe to India.* Rosen, 2003. ISBN: 0-8239-3632-5. Gr. 5-8

Ehrlich, Amy, ed. *When I Was Your Age: Original Stories about Growing Up.* Candlewick, 1996. ISBN: 1-56402-306-0. Gr. 5-8

Fleischman, Sid. *The Abracadabra Kid: A Writer's Life.* Greenwillow Books, 1996. ISBN: 0-688-14859-X. Gr. 6-12

Foa, Emma. *Edward Hopper.* Watts, 2003. ISBN: 0-531-12240-9. Gr. 4-8

Freedman, Russell. *Out of Darkness: The Story of Louis Braille.* Clarion Books, 1997. ISBN: 0-395-77516-7. Gr. 4-6

Gaines, Ann Graham. *Benedict Arnold: Patriot or Traitor?* Enslow, 2001. ISBN: 0-7660-1393-6. Gr. 5-8

Gallagher, Aileen. *Prince Henry the Navigator: Pioneer of Modern Exploration.* Rosen, 2003. ISBN: 0-8239-3621-X. Gr. 5-8

Gherman, Beverly. *Ansel Adams: America's Photographer.* Little, Brown, 2002. ISBN: 0-316-82445-3. Gr. 6-10

———. *Norman Rockwell: Storyteller with a Brush.* Simon & Schuster, 2000. ISBN: 0-689-82001-1. Gr. 4-7

Giblin, James Cross. *Charles A. Lindbergh: A Human Hero.* Clarion, 1997. ISBN: 0-395-63389-3. Gr. 5-9

———. *The Life and Death of Adolf Hitler.* Clarion, 2002. ISBN: 0-395-90371-8. Gr. 7 & up

Greenberg, Jan, and Sandra Jordan. *Action Jackson.* Roaring Brook, 2002. ISBN: 0-7613-1682-5. Gr. 2-6

———. *Frank O. Gehry: Outside In.* DK Paper, 2000. ISBN: 0-7894-2677-3. Gr. 4-7

———. *Romare Bearden: Collage of Memories.* Abrams, 2003. ISBN: 0-8109-4589-4. Gr. 3-9

Harmon, Rod. *American Civil Rights Leaders.* Enslow, 2000. ISBN: 0-7660-1381-2. Gr. 5-7

Heinrichs, Ann. *William Jefferson Clinton.* Compass Point, 2002. ISBN: 0-7565-0207-1. Gr. 4-8

Holland, Gini. *Pablo Picasso.* World Almanac, 2003. ISBN: 0-8368-5084-X. Gr. 5-8

Horn, Geoffrey M. *Steven Spielberg.* World Almanac, 2002. ISBN: 0-8368-5240-0. Gr. 6-9

Howard, Megan. *Christopher Reeve.* Lerner, 1999. ISBN: 0-8225-4945-X. Gr. 6-9

Hughes, Libby. *Nelson Mandela: Voice of Freedom.* iUniverse.com, 2000. ISBN: 0-595-00733-3. Adult

Jimenez, Francisco. *Breaking Through.* Houghton Mifflin, 2002. ISBN: 0-618-34248-6. Gr. 7 & up

———. *The Circuit: Stories from the Life of a Migrant Child.* University of New Mexico Press, 1997. ISBN: 0-8263-1797-9. Gr. 5-9

Johnson, Rebecca. *Ernest Shackleton: Gripped by the Antarctic.* Carolrhoda, 2003. ISBN: 0-87614-920-4. Gr. 6-10

Kallen, Stuart. *Native American Chiefs and Warriors.* Lucent, 1999. ISBN: 1-56006-364-5. Gr. 6-10

Kelley, True. *Pablo Picasso: Breaking All the Rules.* Grosset & Dunlap. 2002. ISBN: 0-448-42879-2. Juv

Koopman, Andy. *Charles Lindbergh.* Gale, 2003. ISBN: 1-59018-245-6. Gr. 7-12

Kraft, Betsy Harvey. *Theodore Roosevelt: Champion of the American Spirit.* Clarion, 2003. ISBN: 0-618-14264-9. Gr. 4-6

Lalicki, Tom. *Spellbinder: The Life of Harry Houdini.* Holiday House, 2000. ISBN: 0-8234-1499-X. Gr. 3-7

Lawlor, Laurie. *Magnificent Voyage: An American Adventurer on Captain James Cook's Final Expedition.* Holiday, 2002. ISBN: 0-8234-1575-9. Gr. 7-12

Leach, Deba Foxley. *I See You I See Myself: The Young Life of Jacob Lawrence.* Hyperion, 2002. ISBN: 0-943044-26-X. Gr. 5-9

Lekuton, Joseph Lemasolai. *Facing the Lion: Growing up Maasai on the African Savanna.* National Geographic, 2003. ISBN: 0-7922-5125-3. Gr. 4-6

Lewin, Ted. *I Was a Teenage Professional Wrestler.* Scholastic, 1993. ISBN: 0-531-05477-2. Gr. 7-12

MacDonald, Andy. *Dropping in with Andy Mac: Life of a Pro Skateboarder.* Simon & Schuster, 2003. ISBN: 0-689-85784-5. Gr. 5-8

Markel, Rita. *Jimi Hendrix.* Lerner, 2001. ISBN: 0-8225-4990-5. Gr. 7-10

Marrin, Albert. *Commander in Chief Abraham Lincoln and the Civil War.* Penguin Group, 2003. ISBN: 0-525-47069-7. Juv

Menard, Valerie. *Alvar Nunez Cabeza de Vaca.* Mitchell Lane, 2002. ISBN: 1-58415-153-6. Gr. 5-7

Middleton, Haydn. *Frank Lloyd Wright.* Heinemann, 2001. ISBN: 1-58810-203-3. Gr. 5-8

Morey, Janet Nomura, and Wendy Dunn. *Famous Hispanic Americans.* Dutton, 1996. ISBN: 0-525-65190-X. Gr. 7-10

Nardo, Don. *Walt Disney.* Lucent, 2000. ISBN: 1-56006-605-9. Gr. 4-8

Nelson, Marilyn. *Carver: A Life in Poems.* Front Street, 1997. ISBN: 1-886910-53-7. Gr. 7 & up

Netzley, Patricia D. *Presidential Assassins.* Lucent, 2000. ISBN: 1-56006-623-7. Gr. 6-9

O'Connor, Barbara. *Leonardo da Vinci: Renaissance Genius.* Carolrhoda, 2002. ISBN: 0-87614-467-9. Gr. 5-8

Oliver, Clare. *Jackson Pollock.* Watts, 2003. ISBN: 0-531-12237-9. Gr. 5-8

Partridge, Elizabeth. *This Land Was Made for You and Me: The Life and Songs of Woodie Guthrie.* Viking, 2002. ISBN: 0-670-03535-1. Gr. 6-12

Paulsen, Gary. *Caught by the Sea.* Delacorte, 2001. ISBN: 0-385-32645-9. Gr. 5-8

———. *Guts: The True Stories Behind Hatchet and the Brian Books.* Delacorte, 2001. ISBN: 0-385-32650-5. Gr. 5-10

Platt, Larry. *Only the Strong Survive: The Odyssey of Allen Iverson.* HarperCollins, 2002. ISBN: 0-06-009773-6. Adult

Reeve, Christopher. *Still Me: A Life.* Ballantine, 1999. ISBN: 0-345-43241-X. Adult

Reiter, Chris. *Thomas Jefferson.* Enslow, 2002. ISBN: 0-7660-5071-8. Gr. 4-7

Roberts, Jeremy. *The Beatles.* Lerner, 2001. ISBN: 0-8225-4998-0. Gr. 5-8

Ross, Michael Elsohn. *Salvador Dali and the Surrealists: Their Lives and Ideas.* Chicago Review, 2003. ISBN: 1- 55652-479-X. YA

Salkeld, Audrey. *Mystery on Everest: A Photobiography of George Mallory.* National Geographic, 2000. ISBN: 0-7922-7222-6. Gr. 5-8

Seate, Mike. *Jesse James: The Man and His Machines.* Motorbooks International, 2003. ISBN: 0-7603-1614-7. Adult

Selfridge, John. *John Coltrane: A Sound Supreme.* Watts, 1999. ISBN: 0-531-11542-9. Gr. 7-12

Shields, Charles J. *Roald Dahl.* Chelsea, 2002. ISBN: 0-7910-6722-X. Gr. 4-7

———. *Spike Lee.* Chelsea, 2002. ISBN: 0-1910-6715-7. Gr. 5-7

Siebold, Thomas, ed. *Martin Luther King, Jr.* Greenhaven, 2000. ISBN: 0-7377-0227-3. Gr. 7-12

Sis, Peter. *The Tree of Life: A Book Depicting the Life of Charles Darwin, Naturalist, Geologist & Thinker.* Farrar, Straus & Giroux, 2003. ISBN: 0-374-45628-3. Gr. 4-6

Spinelli, Jerry. *Knots in My Yo-Yo String: The Autobiography of a Kid.* Knopf, 1998. ISBN: 0-679-98791-6. Gr. 5-9

Stanley, Diane. *Michelangelo.* HarperCollins, 2000. ISBN: 0-688-15086-1. Gr. 5-8

Steffins, Bradley. *J. K. Rowling.* Gale, 2002. ISBN: 1-56006-776-4. Gr. 5-7

Sullivan, George. *Picturing Lincoln: Famous Photographs That Popularized the President.* Clarion, 2000. ISBN: 0-395-91682-8. Gr. 5-8

Thrasher, Thomas. *Gunfighters.* Lucent, 2000. ISBN: 1-56006-570-2. Gr. 6-9

Whiting, Jim. *Junipero Jose Serra.* Mitchell Lane, 2003. ISBN: 1-58415-187-0. Gr. 5-7

Woog, Adam. *Gangsters.* Lucent, 2000. ISBN: 1-56006-638-5. Gr. 6-9

Worth, Richard. *Ponce de Leon and the Age of Spanish Exploration in World History.* Enslow, 2003. ISBN: 0-7660-1940-3. Gr. 5-9

Wren, Laura Lee. *Garth Brooks: Country Music Superstar.* Enslow, 2002. ISBN: 0-7660-1673-2. Gr. 6-10

———. *Pirates and Privateers of the High Seas.* Enslow, 2003. ISBN: 0-7660-1542-4. Gr. 6-10

Wukovits, John. *Tim Allen.* Chelsea, 1998. ISBN: 0-7910-4697-4. Gr. 6-9

Yep, Laurence. *The Lost Garden.* HarperCollins, 1996. ISBN: 0-688-13701-6. Gr. 7 & up

Yoder, Carolyn P., ed. *George Washington: The Writer: A Treasury of Letters, Diaries, and Public Documents.* Boyds Mills, 2003. ISBN: 1-56397-199-2. Gr. 7-10

Zohorsky, Janet R. *Medieval Knights and Warriors.* Gale, 2003. ISBN: 1-56006-954-6. Gr. 6-9

Picture Books

Adler, David. *A Picture Book of Davy Crockett.* Holiday House, 1996. ISBN: 0-8234-1212-1. Juv

Aliki. *The King's Day: Louis XIV of France.* HarperCollins, 1991. ISBN: 0-06-443268-8. Juv

Anaya, Rudolfo. *An Elegy on the Death of Cesar Chavez.* Cinco Puntos, 2000. ISBN: 0-938317-51-2. Juv

Anderson, M.T. *Strange Mr. Satie.* Viking, 2003. ISBN: 0-670-03637-4. Gr. 4-6

Bridges, Ruby. *Through My Eyes.* Scholastic, 1999. ISBN: 0-590-18923-9. Juv

Bruchac, Joseph. *Crazy Horse's Vision.* Lee & Low, 2000. ISBN: 1-880000-94-6. Juv

Burleigh, Robert. *Flight: The Journey of Charles Lindbergh.* Penguin, 1991. ISBN: 0-399-22272-3. Juv

Giblin, James Cross. *George Washington: A Picture Book Biography.* Scholastic, 1998. ISBN: 0-590-48101-0. Juv

———. *Thomas Jefferson: A Picture Book Biography.* Scholastic, 1994. ISBN: 0-590-44838-2. Juv

Kalman, Maira. *Fireboat: The Heroic Adventures of the John J. Harvey.* Putnam, 2002. ISBN: 0-399-23953-7. Juv

King, Martin Luther, Jr. *I Have a Dream.* Scholastic, 1997. ISBN: 0-590-20516-1. Gr. 4 & up

Krull, Kathleen. *Harvesting Hope: The Story of Cesar Chavez.* Harcourt, 2003. ISBN: 0-15-201437-3. Juv

Lasky, Kathryn. *The Librarian Who Measured the Earth.* Little, Brown, 1994. ISBN: 0-316-51526-4. Juv

Loewen, Nancy. *Walt Whitman.* Creative, 1994. ISBN: 0-88682-608-X. Juv

McDonough, Yona Zeldis. *Peaceful Protest: The Life of Nelson Mandela.* Walker, 2002. ISBN: 0-8027-8823-8. Juv

McGill, Alice. *Molly Bannaky.* Houghton, 1999. ISBN: 0-395-72287-X. Juv

Monceaux, Morgan. *Jazz: My Music, My People.* Alfred A. Knopf, 1994. ISBN: 0-679-86518-7. Juv

Myers, Walter Dean. *Malcolm X: A Fire Burning Brightly.* HarperCollins, 2000. ISBN: 0-06-027708-4. Juv

Nichol, Barbara. *Beethoven Lives Upstairs.* Scholastic, 1994. ISBN: 0-531-06828-5. Juv

Niven, Penelope. *Carl Sandburg: Adventures of a Poet.* Harcourt, 2003. ISBN: 0-15-204686-0. Juv

Pinkney, Andrea Davis. *Alvin Ailey.* Disney, 1995. ISBN: 0-7868-1077-7. Juv

———. *Duke Ellington: The Piano Prince and His Orchestra.* Hyperion, 1998. ISBN: 0-7868-0178-6. Juv

Raimondo, Lois. *The Little Lama of Tibet.* Scholastic, 1994. ISBN: 0-590-46167-2. Juv

Rappaport, Doreen. *Martin's Big Words: The Life of Dr. Martin Luther King.* Hyperion, 2001. ISBN: 0-7868-0714-8. Juv

Rodari, Florian. *A Weekend with Picasso.* Rizzoli, 1993. ISBN: 0-8478-1437-8. Juv

Say, Allen. *El Chino.* Houghton Mifflin, 1990. ISBN: 0-395-52023-1. Juv

Sis, Peter. *Tibet: Through the Red Box.* Farrar, Straus & Giroux, 1998. ISBN: 0-374-37552-6. Juv

Skira-Venturi, Rosabianca. *A Weekend with VanGogh.* Rizzoli, 1994. ISBN: 0-8478-1836-5. Juv

Stanlely, Diane. *Bard of Avon: The Story of William Shakespeare.* Morrow Junior Books, 1992. ISBN: 0-688-09109-1. Juv

———. *Charles Dickens: The Man Who Had Great Expectations.* HarperCollins, 1993. ISBN: 0-688-09110-5. Juv

———. *Leonardo da Vinci.* HarperCollins, 1996. ISBN: 0-688-16155-3. Juv

Suen, Anastasia. *Man on the Moon.* Viking, 1997. ISBN: 0-670-87393-4. Juv

Towle, Wendy. *The Real McCoy: The Life of an African-American Inventor.* Scholastic, 1995. ISBN: 0-590-48102-9. Juv

Wiles, Deborah. *Freedom Summer.* Simon & Schuster, 2001. ISBN: 0-689-83016-5. Juv

Winter, Jonah. *Diego.* Turtleback, 1994. ISBN: 0-606-19771-0. Juv

Annotated Journal Article

Lester, Julius. "The Way We Were." *School Library Journal* **(January 2002): 54-57.**
Lester talks about how his childhood has influenced his writing and how even though he writes for children he really is marketing the story to the adults who purchase the books for their children. He has written more than 34 books for children; many of the story ideas come from his childhood or feelings he now has about children today and the uncertainties they face in our troubled times.

9

History

Introduction

Boys like to learn about knights and castles and life in medieval times. They like adventures in the times of westward expansion of our country. They like to read of the ancient times of dinosaurs, woolly mammoths, and even ancient Egypt with its mummies and hieroglyphs. Books like these help them to visualize the past and make a connection. They bring history to life and put meaning to things they have heard or seen on television or in the movies.

Discussion Questions

- How does the information in this book relate to the class text?

- Does this book give you a better understanding of the time period?

- Could this book be made into a movie?

- Is the setting of the story a real place?

- If you could have a conversation with the author, what would you say?

- Are different points of view presented in this book?

- Did you ever feel that you were actually there, that you were part of the story being told?

Annotations

Avi. *Crispin: The Cross of Lead.* **Hyperion Books for Young Children, 2002. ISBN: 0-7868-0828-4. Gr. 3-7**

When his mother died, Crispin, a serf bound to the land, went into the forest to grieve. Afterward, the steward of the manor discovers Crispin and declares him a wolf's head, which means that he may be killed on sight. Crispin escapes, but his enemies continue to follow him. The clue to his heritage lies in the lead cross that belonged to his mother and was inscribed by her. This is a mystery to Crispin since he cannot read and did not know that his mother could read and write. Who were his mother and father, and why is he being pursued? Will the juggler he meets teach him all that he needs to keep him safe? Winner of the Newbery award.

Bartoletti, Susan Campell. *Kids on Strike!* **Houghton Mifflin Company, 1999. ISBN: 0-395-88892-1. Gr. 4-7**

Children can make a difference. The author traces the working conditions and the steps children took to bolster their civil rights in the 19th and 20th centuries. Black-and-white photographs document their contributions and arduous journey. Nonfiction.

Blackwood, Gary. *The Year of the Hangman.* **Penguin Putnam Books for Young Readers, 2002. ISBN: 0-525-46921-4. Gr. 9 & up**

Creighton Brown is abducted and taken to a ship bound for the colonies. Creighton will learn that it was his mother who placed Creighton in the custody of her brother, Colonel Gower. This book addresses the question, what if George Washington was in custody and the leaders of the American Revolution were expelled from the colonies? Creighton meets many of the leaders and is pulled between spying for his uncle and the British and his new-found loyalty to the Americans and their fight for freedom.

Bruchac, Joseph. *The Journal of Jesse Smoke: A Cherokee Boy: Trail of Tears, 1838.* **Scholastic, 2001. ISBN: 0-439-12197-3. Gr. 4-8**

The Cherokee Nation is reduced to a small portion of where the present states of Georgia, Tennessee, and North Carolina come together. Now the United States government wants to move these hard-working and industrious people west of the Mississippi. This is Jesse Smoke's diary of events leading up to and during the forced removal to Oklahoma, known as the Trail of Tears, and the death of one-fourth of the Cherokee people.

Curtis, Christopher Paul. *The Watsons Go to Birmingham—1963: A Novel.* **Delacorte Press, 1995. ISBN: 0-385-32175-9. Gr. 4-7**

A story narrated by Kenny, age nine, about his middle-class black family, the Weird Watsons of Flint, Michigan. When Kenny's 13-year-old brother, Byron, gets to be too much trouble, they head south to Birmingham to visit Grandma, the one person who can shape him up. And they happen to be in Birmingham when Grandma's church is blown up

Fradin, Dennis Brindell. *Bound for the North Star: True Stories of Fugitive Slaves.* **Clarion Books, 2000. ISBN: 0-395-97017-2. Gr. 7-12**

In 1776 there were 500,000 slaves in the 13 colonies. Fifty thousand slaves escaped the South and fled to the North and Canada. These stories tell about the desperate conditions the slaves endured in their quest for freedom. Slavery still exists; "the UN estimates that 100 million children around the world live in bondage." Nonfiction.

Gundisch, Karin. *How I Became an American.* **Cricket Books, 2001. ISBN: 0-8126-4875-7. Gr. 3-7**

This winner of the Batchelder Award follows the journey of a family emigrating from Germany to America during the early 1900s. Mama asks Johann to write everything down so that they will never forget. Johann's father and eldest brother leave for Youngstown, Ohio, first and later send for the rest of the family. The journey is long and hard and life in Youngstown is not easy. The children of the family are able to adapt to the new lifestyle easier than the parents. Johann "relays the many differences between the two lifestyles and cultures."

Hurst, Carol Otis, and Rebecca Otis. *A Killing in Plymouth Colony.* **Houghton Mifflin, 2003. ISBN: 0-618-27597-5. Gr. 5-9**

In 1630, a man was murdered for the first time in Plymouth Colony. This historical novel is based on people who lived in the colony, and it is the author's interpretation of what might have happened. John Bradford, son of Governor Bradford, was eight years old when he joined his father and stepmother in the colony and is eleven when the murder takes place. Governor Bradford is a stern man, and young John does not know how to relate to him. John Billington is a drunkard, and the governor is quick to blame him for any problem that arises in the colony. The murder is no different. Young John Bradford thinks his father sees him the same way he sees John Billington. Neither one can do anything right, and both are outcasts.

Lasky, Kathryn. *The Man Who Made Time Travel.* **Farrar, Straus & Giroux, 2003. ISBN: 0-374-34788-3. Gr. 4-6**

Before people could accurately measure the latitude and longitude of their ship's position, many lives and ships were lost. The reason they could not measure their latitude and longitude was that no one had not yet perfected a clock that was accurate and reliable not only on land but at sea. In 1714, Britain established the Longitude Prize of £20,000, or $12 million in today's currency. It would take John Harrison until he was 79 and the creation of five clocks, H1, H2, H3, H4, and H5 until he was awarded the remaining prize money in 1773. In spite of this, he was never named the official prizewinner. Picture book.

Lester, Julius. *John Henry.* **Penguin Paper, 1999. ISBN: 0-14-056622-8. Juv**

Julius Lester retells the original African-American ballad of John Henry, a man with unusual strength who challenges a steam drill in digging through the Allegheny Mountains in West Virginia. A Caldecott Honor Book. Picture book.

Murphy, Jim. *An American Plague: The True and Terrifying Story of the Yellow Fever Epidemic of 1793.* **Clarion Books, 2003. ISBN: 0-395-77608-2. Gr. 5-9**

In 1793, Philadelphia was the temporary capital of the United States. On Saturday, August 3, a young sailor died after a high fever and violent seizures. By August 28, the fever was everywhere, the government was all but shut down, and thousands of people had left town. Those who remained behind were either too poor or had nowhere else to go. The cures for yellow fever were varied and based upon tradition, folk medicines, and medical practice of the times such as bloodletting. By the end of October, the disease seemed to be declining, but the inhabitants were encouraged "to clean their homes thoroughly, burn gunpowder to purify the air, dump lime down their privies, and whitewash every room." Nonfiction.

Nieuwsma, Milton J. *Kinderlager: An Oral History of Young Holocaust Survivors.* **Holiday House, 1998. ISBN: 0-8234-1358-6. Gr. 4-7**

Kinderlager was a special section of the Auschwitz-Birkenau concentration camp that housed the children. This book documents the lives of three of these children: before the war, life in the concentration camp, liberation by the Soviets, and after the war. At the time of the Soviet liberation the world did not take much notice of this tragedy. This is the true story of three of the youngest survivors of Kinderlager. Nonfiction.

Park, Linda Sue. *A Single Shard.* **Clarion Books, 2001. ISBN: 0-395-97827-0. Gr. 5-9**

A Single Shard is a humble story of perseverance, patience, and courage. The story takes place during the 12th century in a potter's village in Korea. Tree-ear is orphaned at a young age and is brought to the village of Ch'ulp'o to live with an uncle. When he arrives the uncle dies of the fever, and Tree-ear is brought to Crane-man, who takes care of him temporarily. Tree-ear remains with Crane-man and lives under the bridge; they survive by their wiles and frugalness. Tree-ear is fascinated by the potter Min and observes him, unbeknownst to Min. One day when Tree-ear is bold enough to pick up one of the unfired pieces, Min startles him and the boy drops the piece; thus begins Tree-ear's debt, which led to him working long and hard for Min with hopes of becoming a potter one day.

Tillage, Leon Walter. *Leon's Story.* **Farrar, Straus & Giroux, 1997. ISBN: 0-374-34379-9. Gr. 3-7**

This is the story of Leon Walter Tillage as spoken on tape to Susan L. Roth. Leon currently works as a custodian at the Park School in Baltimore, Maryland, where he gives a speech about his life as a part of the curriculum. Leon was the son of a sharecropper and grew up in North Carolina in the 1940s. His life was about hard work and getting an education in an inferior school, about walking home from school, and about being passed by the white kids on the bus, who would holler and call names. When this happened, the black children would run and try to hide, but sometimes the bus stopped and the white kids would get off and throw stones at whomever they could. Leon witnessed his father being intentionally run over and killed by some drunken white teenagers, who were never punished for their actions. "In those days, Blacks didn't have any voice at all, and there was no such thing as taking the white man to court. You couldn't vote; you weren't even considered a citizen." Nonfiction.

Turner, Ann. *Drummer Boy: Marching to the Civil War.* **HarperCollins, 1998. ISBN: 0-06-027696-7. Juv**

A young boy is influenced by Abraham Lincoln, lies about his age, and joins the Northern side of the Civil War. He becomes a drummer boy to help put spirit into the soldiers. The individual battles begin to run together, and he sees "things no boy should ever see." Picture book.

Wells, Rosemary. *Wingwalker.* **Hyperion, 2002. ISBN: 0-7868-0397-5. Gr. 3-6**

In this short fiction book, Ruben wins a chance to ride in the passenger seat of a two-seat plane. Afterward Ruben vows he will not go higher than his attic window, if only God will keep him away from airplanes. The rest of the story tells how Ruben's family is forced to leave Ambler, Oklahoma, during the Depression, and how it came to be that Ruben stood on the wing of the Land of Cotton and for one moment was a wingwalker.

Yep, Laurence. *The Traitor: Golden Mountain Chronicles, 1885.* **HarperCollins, 2003. ISBN: 0-06-027522-7. Gr. 5-8**

This continuation of the Golden Mountain Chronicles is told from alternating viewpoints of Joseph Young, a lonely Chinese boy, and Michael Purdy, a lonely American boy. Both are outcasts and victims of bullies from town. They accidentally meet in a cave that Joseph discovers and quickly form a friendship. As the relations between the townspeople and the Chinese miners deteriorate, both boys seek refuge at Star Rock. Neither boy feels he belongs in his own community. The Westerners blame the Chinese for all of their trouble. They come together as a mob, riot, kill the Chinese, and burn their homes. Joseph and his father seek sanctuary in Michael's house. This story is based on actual events.

Yin. *Coolies*. Philomel Books, 2001. ISBN: 0-399-23227-3. Juv

In the mid-1800s Shek and his little brother Wong left China for the new land, America. The Chinese laborers were hired to build railroad tracks east to meet up with the Irish laborers who were building tracks west. The called the Chinese "coolies," lowly workers. Four years later, after many hardships, east met the west, and the two brothers took their savings and rode to San Francisco with the prospect of bringing their family over from China. Picture book.

Yolen, Jane, and Heidi Elisabeth Yolen Stemple. *Roanoke: The Lost Colony: An Unsolved Mystery from History*. Simon & Schuster, 2003. ISBN: 0-689-82321-5. Juv

In 1587, 92 new colonists left England for the new world: 60 men, 20 women, and 12 children. The previous colonists at Roanoke were not prepared and had problems with the Native Americans, so they returned to England. Soldiers remained at the fort in anticipation of the new group of colonists. When the new group arrived, led by John White, no soldiers were around, only a single skeleton. The colonists had not planned on staying in Roanoke, but there was no other option. White was pressured to go back to England to get supplies and soldiers. When he returned three years later the colony was empty and the colonists gone. The authors propose five common theories of what might have happened and leave it up to readers to draw their own conclusions or propose a new theory.

Bibliography

Almond, David. *Counting Stars*. Delacorte, 2002. ISBN: 0-385-90034-1. Gr. 5-9

Ambrose, Stephen E. *This Vast Land: A Young Man's Journal of the Lewis and Clark Expedition.* Simon & Schuster, 2003. ISBN: 0-689-86448-5. YA

Armistead, John. *The Return of Gabriel*. Milkweed, 2002. ISBN: 1-57131-637-X. Gr. 6-9

Atres, Katherine. *Macaroni Boy*. Delacorte, 2003. ISBN: 0-385-73016-0. Gr. 5-8

Banks, Lynne Reid. *The Dungeon*. HarperCollins, 2002. ISBN: 0-06-623782-3. Gr. 6-9

Banks, Sara Harrell. *Abraham's Battle: A Novel of Gettysburg*. Simon & Schuster, 1999. ISBN: 0-689-81779-7. Gr. 4-8

Blackwood, Gary. *Shakespeare's Spy*. Penguin, 2003. ISBN: 0-525-47145-6. Gr. 3-7

Brooke, Peggy. *Jake's Orphan*. DK Paper, 2000. ISBN: 0-7894-2628-5. Gr. 7-10

Bruchac, Joseph. *The Arrow over the Door*. Dial, 1998. ISBN: 0-8037-2078-5. Gr. 4-7

———. *The Winter People*. Dial, 2002. ISBN: 0-8037-2694-5. Gr. 6-10

Butler, Amy. *Virginia Bound*. Clarion, 2003. ISBN: 0-618-24752-1. Gr. 4-7

Cadnum, Michael. *Forbidden Forest*. Scholastic, 2002. ISBN: 0-43931774-6. Gr. 7-10

———. *Raven of the Waves.* Scholastic, 2001. ISBN: 0-531-30334-9. Gr. 7-10

Calvert, Patricia. *Betrayed.* Simon & Schuster, 2000. ISBN: 0-689-83472-1. Gr. 5-8

Carbone, Elisa. *Storm Warriors.* Knopf, 2001. ISBN: 0-375-90664-9. Gr. 4-8

———. *The True Prince.* Knopf, 2002. ISBN: 0-375-81433-7. Gr. 7-10

Chen, Da. *Wandering Warrior.* Delacorte, 2003. ISBN: 0-385-73020-9. Gr. 8-12

Collier, James Lincoln. *Wild Boy.* Marshall Cavendish, 2002. ISBN: 0-7614-5126-9. Gr. 5-8

Crist-Evans, Craig. *Moon Over Tennessee: A Boy's Civil War Journal.* Houghton Mifflin, 1999. ISBN: 0-395-91208-3. Gr. 4-6

Crossley-Holland, Kevin. *The Seeing Stone.* Scholastic, 2001. ISBN: 0-439-26326-3. Gr. 5-8

Crowe, Chris. *Mississippi Trial.* Penguin Putnam, 2002. ISBN: 0-8037-2745-3. Gr. 7-12

Crowley, Bridget. *Feast of Fools.* Simon & Schuster, 2003. ISBN: 0-689-86512-0. Gr. 6-9

Curtis, Christopher Paul. *Bud, Not Buddy.* Delacorte, 1999. ISBN: 0-385-32306-9. Gr. 4-7

D'Adamo, Francesco. *Iqbal.* Atheneum, 2003. ISBN: 0-689-85445-5. Gr. 4-6

Denenberg, Barry. *The Journal of William Thomas Emerson: A Revolutionary War Patriot: Boston, Massachusetts, 1774.* Scholastic, 1998. ISBN: 0-590-31350-9. Gr. 5-8

Dickinson, Peter. *Suth's Story.* Grosset, 1998. ISBN: 0-399-23327-X. Gr. 4-7

Durbin, William. *The Journal of C. J. Jackson: A Dust Bowl Migrant, Oklahoma to California, 1935.* Scholastic, 2002. ISBN: 0-439-15306-9. Gr. 4-7

———. *The Journal of Otto Peltonen: A Finnish Immigrant.* Scholastic, 2000. ISBN: 0-439-009254-X. Gr. 6-12

Geras, Adele. *Troy.* Harcourt, 2002. ISBN: 0-15-204570-8. Gr. 9 & up

Gregory, Kristiana. *Orphan Runaways.* Scholastic, 1998. ISBN: 0-590-60366-3. Gr. 5-7

Hahn, Mary Downing. *Hear the Wind Blow: A Novel of the Civil War.* Houghton, 2003. ISBN: 0-618-18190-3. Gr. 5-9

———. *Promises to the Dead.* Clarion, 2000. ISBN: 0-395-96394-X. Gr. 5-9

Harlow, Joan Hiatt. *Joshua's Song.* Simon & Schuster, 2001. ISBN: 0-689-84119-1. Gr. 5-8

Harrar, George. *The Trouble with Jeremy Chance.* Milkweed, 2003. ISBN: 1-57131-647-7. Gr. 4-7

Harris, Carol Flynn. *A Place for Joey.* Boyds Mills, 2001. ISBN: 1-56397-108-9. Gr. 4-8

Haugaard, Eric C. *The Samurai's Tale.* Houghton Mifflin, 1984. ISBN: 0-395-54970-1. Gr. 7-12

Hesse, Karen. *Stowaway.* Simon & Schuster, 2002. ISBN: 0-689-83989-8. Gr. 5-9

Hoobler, Dorothy and Thomas Hoobler. *The Demon in the Teahouse.* Putnam, 2001. ISBN: 0-399-23499-3. Gr. 7-9

Horowitz, Anthony. *The Devil and His Boy.* Putnam, 2000. ISBN: 0-399-23432-2. Gr. 5-8

Hughes, Pat. *Guerilla Season.* Farrar, Straus & Giroux, 20003. ISBN: 0-374-32811-0. Gr. 6 & up

Jennings, Patrick. *The Wolving Time.* Scholastic, 2003. ISBN: 0-439-39555-0. Gr. 6-10

Jinks, Catherine. *Pagan's Crusade.* Candlewick, 2003. ISBN: 0-7636-2019-X. YA

Jung, Reinhardt. *Dreaming in Black & White.* Penguin Group, 2003. ISBN: 0-8037-2811-5. Gr. 4-6

Karr, Kathleen. *The Boxer.* Farrar, Straus & Giroux, 2000. ISBN: 0-374-30921-3. Gr. 6-9

———. *The 7th Knot.* Marshall Cavendish, 2003. ISBN: 0-7614-5135-8. Gr. 6-9

Lawrence, Iain. *The Buccaneers.* Delacorte, 2001. ISBN: 0-385-32736-6. Gr. 5-8

———. *The Wreckers.* Bantam Doubleday Dell, 1999. ISBN: 0-440-41545-4. Gr. 5-8

Lester, Julius. *To Be a Slave.* Sagebrush Education, 2000. ISBN: 0-613-33732-8. Gr. 5-8

Levine, Gail C. *Dave at Night.* HarperCollins, 1999. ISBN: 0-06-028154-5. Gr. 5-9

Levitin, Sonia. *Clem's Chances.* Scholastic, 2001. ISBN: 0-439-29314-6. Gr. 4-7

———. *The Cure.* HarperCollins, 2000. ISBN: 0-380-73298-X. Gr. 7 & up

Lisson, Deborah. *Red Hugh.* O'Brien Paper, 2001. ISBN: 0-86278-604-5. Gr. 6-12

Lynch, Chris. *Gold Dust.* HarperCollins, 2000. ISBN: 0-06-028175-8. Gr. 5 & up

Massie, Elizabeth. *1870: Not with Our Blood.* Tor Paper, 2000. ISBN: 0-312-59092-9. Gr. 6-9

McCaughrean, Geraldine. *Casting the Gods Adrift: A Tale of Ancient Egypt.* Cricket, 2003. ISBN: 0-8126-2684-2. Gr. 5-8

———. *The Kite Rider.* HarperCollins, 2002. ISBN: 0-06-623875-7. Gr. 7 & up

———. *The Pirate's Son.* Scholastic, 1998. ISBN: 0-590-20344-4. Gr. 7-10

Moore, Robin. *The Man with the Silver Oar.* HarperCollins, 2002. ISBN: 0-380-97877-6. Gr. 6-12

Murphy, Jim. *The Journal of James Edmond Pease: A Civil War Union Soldier, Virginia, 1863.* Scholastic, 1998. ISBN: 0-590-43814-X. Gr. 4-8

Myers, Anna. *Stolen by the Sea.* Walker, 2001. ISBN: 0-8027-8787-8. Gr. 5-8

———. *Tulsa Burning.* Walker, 2002. ISBN: 0-8027-8829-7. Gr. 8-10

Myers, Walter Dean. *The Journal of Joshua Loper: A Black Cowboy.* Scholastic, 1999. ISBN: 0-590-02691-7. Gr. 5-8

Napoli, Donna Jo. *Breath.* Atheneum, 2003. ISBN: 0-689-86174-5. YA

Osborne, Mary Pope. *My Brother's Keeper: Virginia's Civil War Diary, Gettysburg, Pennsylvania, 1863.* Scholastic, 2000. ISBN: 0-439-15307-7. Gr. 4-7

Park, Linda Sue. *The Kite Fighters.* Clarion, 2000. ISBN: 0-395-94041-9. Gr. 5-7

———. *When My Name Was Keoko.* Clarion, 2002. ISBN: 0-618-13335-6. Gr. 5-9

Paterson, Katherine. *Jip: His Story.* Puffin Paper, 1998. ISBN: 0-14-038674-2. Gr. 5-9

Paulsen, Gary. *Tucket's Home.* Delacorte, 2000. ISBN: 0-385-32648-3. Gr. 4-8

Pearsall, Shelley. *Trouble Don't Last.* Knopf, 2002. ISBN: 0-375-81490-6. Gr. 5-10

Rinaldi, Ann. *The Journal of Jasper Jonathan Pierce: A Pilgrim Boy, Plymouth.* Scholastic, 2000. ISBN: 0-590-51978-9. Gr. 4-8

Rubalcaba, Jill. *The Wadjet Eye.* Clarion, 2000. ISBN: 0-395-68942-2. Gr. 5-8

Salisbury, Graham. *Under the Blood Red Sun.* Random House, 1995. ISBN: 0-614-97639-1. Gr. 7 & up

Seely, Debra. *Grasslands.* Holiday, 2002. ISBN: 0-8234-1731-X. Gr. 5-8

Skurzynski, Gloria. *Rockbuster.* Simon & Schuster, 2001. ISBN: 0-689-83991-X. Gr. 6-12

Spinelli, Jerry. *Milkweed.* Knopf, 2003. ISBN: 0-375-81374-8. Gr. 7 & up

Spooner, Michael. *Daniel's Walk.* Holt, 2001. ISBN: 0-8050-6750-7. Gr. 6-9

Springer, Nancy. *I Am Mordred: A Tale from Camelot.* Putnam, 1998. ISBN: 0-399-23143-9. Gr. 7-12

Stowe, Cynthia. *The Second Escape of Arthur Cooper.* Marshall Cavendish, 2000. ISBN: 0-7614-5069-6. Gr. 5-7

Strickland, Brad, and Thomas E. Fuller. *Heart of Steele.* Simon & Schuster, 2003. ISBN: 0-689-85298-3. Gr. 5-8

Taylor, Mildred D. *The Land.* Penguin Putnam, 2001. ISBN: 0-8037-1950-7. Gr. 7-12

Torrey, Michele. *To the Edge of the World.* Knopf, 2003. ISBN: 0-375-82338-7. Gr. 5-8

Trottier, Maxine. *Under a Shooting Star.* Stoddart Paper, 2002. ISBN: 0-7737-6228-0. Gr. 5-8

Wait, Lea. *Seaward Born.* Simon & Schuster, 2003. ISBN: 0-689-84719-X. Gr. 4-7

Whitesel, Cheryl Aylward. *Rebel: A Tibetan Odyssey.* HarperCollins, 2000. ISBN: 0-688-16735-7. Gr. 5-8

Wilson, Diane Lee. *To Ride the Gods' Own Stallion.* DK Ink., 2000. ISBN: 0-7894-6802-6. Gr. 6-8

Yee, Paul. *Dead Man's Gold and Other Stories.* Groundwood, 2002. ISBN: 0-88899-475-3. Gr. 6 & up

Yep, Laurence. *Dragon's Gate: Golden Mountain Chronicles: 1867.* HarperCollins, 1995. ISBN: 0-06-440489-7. Gr. 7 & up

———. *The Journal of Wong Ming-Chung.* Scholastic, 2000. ISBN: 0-590-38607-7. Gr. 4-7

———. *Sea Glass: Golden Mountain Chronicles: 1970.* HarperCollins, 2002. ISBN: 0-06-441003-X. Gr. 5 & up

———. *Thief of Hearts: Golden Mountain Chronicles: 1995.* HarperCollins, 1997. ISBN: 0-06-440591-5. Gr. 5 & up

Yolen, Jane. *Sword of the Rightful King.* Harcourt, 2003. ISBN: 0-15-202527-8. Gr. 6-9

Nonfiction

Campbell, Susan. *Black Potatoes: The Story of the Great Irish Famine 1845–1850.* Houghton Mifflin, 2001. ISBN: 0-618-54883-1. Gr. 5-9

Cox, Clinton. *Come All You Brave Soldiers: Blacks in the Revolutionary War.* Scholastic, 1999. ISBN: 0-590-47576-2. Gr. 6-9

Crowe, Chris. *Getting Away with Murder: The True Story of the Emmett Till Case.* Penguin Group, 2003. ISBN: 0-8037-2804-2. Gr. 8-12

Feelings, Tom. *The Middle Passage: White Ships/Black Cargo.* Penguin Group, 1995. ISBN: 0-8037-1804-7. Juv

Freedman, Russell. *In the Days of the Vaqueros: America's First True Cowboys.* Houghton Mifflin, 2001. ISBN: 0-395-96788-0. Juv

Hoose, Phillip. *We Were There Too!: Young People in U.S. History.* Farrar, Straus & Giroux, 2001. ISBN: 0-374-38252-2. Gr. 4-7

Murphy, Jim. *Inside the Alamo.* Delacorte, 2003. ISBN: 0-385-32574-6. Gr. 3-7

Stanley, Jerry. *Cowboys and Longhorns: A Portrait of the Long Drive.* Crown, 2003. ISBN: 0-375-81565-1. Gr. 9-12

Winters, Kay. *Voices of Ancient Egypt.* National Geographic, 2003. ISBN: 0-7922-7560-8. Gr. 2-6

Picture Books

Bartone, Elisa. *Peppe the Lamplighter.* HarperCollins, 1993. ISBN: 0-688-10268-9. Juv

Bowen, Gary. *Stranded at Plimoth Plantation 1626.* HarperCollins, 1994. ISBN: 0-06-022541-6. Juv

Hall, Donald. *The Ox-Cart Man.* Penguin, 1983. ISBN: 0-14-050441-9. Juv

Kurtz, Jane. *River Friendly, River Wild.* Simon & Schuster, 2000. ISBN: 0-689-82049-6. Juv

Lester, Julius. *From Slave Ship to Freedom Road.* Dial, 1998. ISBN: 0-8037-1893-4. Juv

Lewin, Ted. *Red Legs: A Drummer Boy of the Civil War.* HarperCollins, 2001. ISBN: 0-688-16024-7. Juv

Littlesugar, Amy. *Freedom School, Yes!* Philomel, 2001. ISBN: 0-399-23006-8. Juv

McDonald, Megan. *The Potato Man.* Orchard, 1991. ISBN: 0-531-05914-6. Juv

McGugan, Jim. *Josepha: A Prairie Boy's Story.* Sagebrush Education Resources, 1998. ISBN: 0-613-81280-8. Juv

Miller, William. *Richard Wright and the Library Card.* Lee & Low, 1997. ISBN: 1-880000-57-1. Juv

Siy, Alexander. *Footprints on the Moon.* Charlesbridge, 2001. ISBN: 1-57091-408-7. Juv

Skarmeta, Antonio. *The Composition.* Groundwood, 2000. ISBN: 0-88899-390-0. Juv

Stolz, Mary. *Zekmet, the Stone Carver: A Tale of Ancient Egypt.* Harcourt, 1997. ISBN: 0-15-201601-5. Juv

Wiles, Deborah, *Freedom Summer.* Simon & Schuster, 2001. ISBN: 0-689-83016-5. Juv

Winter, Jannette. *Follow the Drinking Gourd.* Sagebrush Education Resources, 1992. ISBN: 0-8335-8047-7. Juv

Yolen, Jane. *Encounter.* Harcourt, 1996. ISBN: 0-15-201389-X. Juv

Annotated Journal Article

Albright, Lettie and Sylvia Vardell. "1950 to 2000 in Picture Books." *Book Links* **(September 2003): 25.**

This article reviews picture books for older readers that tell the human side of some events in history. These books give a visual picture and a clearer understanding to an event that might be described in one short paragraph in a history/social studies textbook. These books can be used to introduce a topic, provide an overview, help students see multiple points of view, and develop critical thinking skills. The article reviews 24 picture books and has a special section about Eve Bunting and her work with contemporary social issues.

10

Graphic Novels

Introduction

Graphic novels are full-length original stories written in comic book format but presented in book form. They feature the sequential art that is highlighted in comics. The format is totally visual, showing the story unfolding in panels of graphics and short text across the page. Graphic novels cover all genres. Many teachers and librarians find it difficult to allow graphic novels in the classroom or library because they do not think of them as literature. Graphic novels of today have sophisticated storylines and more advanced artwork than the comic books of days of old. But they also can have explicit language and intense violence, so they must be scrutinized carefully before being placed in the hands of readers.

Annotated Professional Resource

Lyga, Allyson A. W., with Barry Lyga. *Graphic Novels in Your Media Center: A Definitive Guide.* Libraries Unlimited, 2004. ISBN 1-59158-142-7.

> This is such an important and useful guide that it is being featured in this chapter. It contains all the information you need to successfully integrate graphic novels into the media center and the classroom! The first section, about visual literacy and reluctant readers, discusses students who are incapable of visualization and those who are dependent on visuals. There is also a section on getting teachers interested in graphic novels and making curricular connections. Graphic novels provide high interest because of pop culture. The next part explains the difference between comic books and

graphic novels, explores some of the related terminology, and even presents information on how to read a comic book! The authors offer an annotated list of appropriate graphic novel titles for elementary, middle, and high school collections. They give suggestions for dealing with resistance from teachers and provide ideas on how to make connections with comic book stores. There is a special section for librarians about adding graphic novels to the collection. For teachers there are 17 actual lesson plans for using graphic novels. The appendix provides a list of 100 graphic novels. This is an excellent resource for equipping boys and reluctant readers with a new type of book that may just be the key to getting them interested in reading.

Discussion Questions

- Could this graphic novel be made into a movie?

- Describe the quality of the artwork. Does it enhance the story?

- Was the text difficult?

- Was the topic interesting?

- Would you look for traditional books on this same topic?

- Was the story a "page-turner" or just a regular story?

- Does this format make it easier to read?

- Have you read other graphic novels? If so, which one is your favorite, so far?

Annotations

Kobayashi, Makoto, *What's Michael?* Dark Horse Manga, 2004. ISBN: 1-59307-120-5. Juv
A collection of comics about Michael, who has been described as "Japan's version of Garfield, Heathcliff, and Krazy Kat all rolled into one." The comics include "The Cat Growth" (of mini-mike), "The Ugly Kitten" (who was really a dog), "Urashima Bean-O" (a fable with a twist), "The Count," and "Jiro" (who is a catnip-aholic).

Naifeh, Ted. *Courtney Crumin and the Night Things*. Oni Press, 2002. ISBN: 1-929998-42-2. Juv
Courtney Crumin and her parents move into elderly Aloysius Crumin's mansion, where rumors abound about what goes on inside. Courtney's first day at school is a disaster when she is confronted by some students and they steal her allowance money. Courtney seeks revenge on the leader of her classmates who tormented her. At night when Courtney is unable to sleep, she quietly enters her uncle's library. She reads his 400-year-old books and then uses magic to alter events in her favor until she is strong enough to take care of herself.

Spiegelman, Art. *Maus: A Survivor's Tale: My Father Bleeds History.* **Pantheon Books, 1986. ISBN 0-394-74723-2. Adult**

Author and cartoonist Art Speigelman interviews his father, Vladek, for a book he is writing about his father's survival in Poland from 1936 through the war years. In the graphic novel, the mice are the Jews, the cats are the Nazis, and the pigs are the Poles. The story moves from his father's unhappy present circumstances to the gradual deterioration of his comfortable life in Poland. Vladek married into a wealthy family and was in the Polish army and captured as a war prisoner. He was released as a war prisoner and volunteered for labor assignment to a big German company. Thus began Vladek's struggle to survive through his cleverness, wealth, and family connections. All the time he was struggling to live because to die was easy. At the end of Maus, his father and mother have just arrived at Camp Auschwitz. Most of their family is already dead, including their young son. *Maus II: And Here My Troubles Began*, begins with life in the barracks of the concentration camp.

***Star Wars**: Clone Wars, Volume 3, Last Stand on Jabiim.* **Dark Horse Books, 2004. ISBN: 1-59307-006-3. Adult**

The Jedi forces are a day's trek from the shelter base, and they fear the Confederacy will attack once they find their weak spot. Thirty-seven days of rain and the Force pushes on to the cobalt station, where they plan to be evacuated. The Separatists have just received reinforcements, and their orders are to make the Jedi suffer. The Force is between the planned evacuation and the Separatists. Anakin Skywalker has been ordered to leave and oversee the evacuation, but he does not want to abandon his friends in the upcoming battle.

Tezuka, Osamu. *Astro Boy.* **Dark Horse Manga, 2003. ISBN: 1-56971-899-7. Adult**

This is the final volume of Astro Boy, and it features many short comics from the 1970s and 1980s. Astro Boy flies and helps right the situation when called upon and is a champion of justice, like Superman.

Bibliography

Asimiya, Kia. *Dark Angel: The Path to Destiny.* CPM Comics Paper, 2000. ISBN: 1-56219-827-7. Gr. 8-12

Augustyn, Brian, et al. *Out There: The Evil Within.* DC Comics, 2002. ISBN: 1-56389-893-4. Adult

Avi. *City of Light, City of Dark: A Comic Book Novel.* Orchard, 1995. ISBN: 0-531-07058-1. Gr. 6-9

Bedard, Tony, et al. *Route 666 Traveler: Highway of Horror.* Cross Generation Comics, 2003. ISBN: 1-59314-041-X. YA

Bendis, Brian-Michael, et al. *Ultimate Spider-Man: Power and Responsibility.* Marvel Books, 2001. ISBN: 0-7851-0786-X. Adult

Brennan, Michael. *Electric Girl.* Mighty Gremlin, 2000. ISBN: 0-9703555-0-5. YA

Dini, Paul. *The Batman Adventures: Dangerous Dames and Demons.* DC Comics, 2003. ISBN: 1-56389-973-6. Gr. 6-12

Dison, Chuck. *Way of the Rats: The Walls of Zumar.* CrossGeneration Paper, 2003. ISBN: 1-931484-51-1. Gr. 7-12

Fyqua, Jonathon Scott. *In the Shadow of Edgar Allan Poe.* DC Comics, 2002. ISBN: 1-56389-928-0. Adult

Gaiman, Neil. *Sandman.* Morrow, 2002. ISBN: 0-380-81770-5. Adult

Hinds, Gareth. *Bearskin: A Grimm Tale.* The Comic.Com, 1998. ISBN: 1-893131-00-9. Adult

London, Jack. *Graphic Classics: Jack London.* Eureka Paper, 2003. ISBN: 0-9712464-5-9. Gr. 5-8

Loeb, Jeph. *Batman: Hush, Vol 1.* DC Comics, 2003. ISBN: 1-40120-613-7. Gr. 6 & up

McCloud, Scott. *The New Adventure of Abraham Lincoln.* Homage Comics Paper, 1998. ISBN: 1-887-27987-3. Gr. 7-10

Miller, Frank. *Batman: The Dark Knight Returns.* DC Comics, 2002. ISBN: 1-56389-341-X. Adult

———. *Batman: The Dark Knight Strikes Again.* DC Comics, 2002. ISBN: 1-56389-844-6. Adult

Miller, Mark, et al. *Ultimate X-Men: The Tomorrow People.* Marvel Books, 2001. ISBN: 0785107886. Juv

Mizuno, Ryo. *Record of Lodoss War: The Grey Witch—Birth of a New Knight.* CPM, 2000. ISBN: 1-5621-9928-5. Adult

Moore, Alan. *Watchman.* DC Comics, 1995. ISBN: 0-930289-23-4. Adult

Nishiyama, Yuriko. *Harlem Beat.* TokyoPop, 1999. ISBN: 1-892-21304-4. Gr. 8-12

Ottaviani, Jim. *Dignifying Science: Stories about Women Scientists.* G. T. Labs, 2003. ISBN: 0-9660106-4-7. Gr. 4 & up

———. *Two-Fisted Science.* G. T. Labs, 2001. ISBN: 0-9660106-2-0. Gr. 4-7

Rabagliati, Michel. *Paul Has a Summer Job.* Drawn & Quarterly Books, 2003. ISBN: 1-896597-54-8. Adult

Rapael, Jordan, and Tom Spurgeon. *Stan Lee and the Rise and Fall of the American Comic Book.* Chicago Review Press, 2003. ISBN: 1-5535-2506-0. Gr. 7 & up

Seto, Andy. *Crouching Tiger, Hidden Dragon.* ComicsOne Paper, 2002. ISBN: 1-58899-999-8. Gr. 7-12

Sfar, Joann. *Little Vampire Does Kung Fu!* Simon & Schuster, 2003. ISBN: 0-689-85769-1. Gr. 4-7

Shanower, Eric. *Age of Bronze: A Thousand Ships.* Image Comics Paper, 2001. ISBN: 1-58240-200-0. Gr. 8-12

Slott, Dan, et al. *Justice League Adventures.* DC Comics Paper, 2003. ISBN: 1-56389-954-X. Gr. 5-8

Smith, Jeff. *Bone Volume 1: Out from Boneville.* Cartoon Books, 1996. ISBN: 0-9636609-4-2. Adult

Templeton, Ty. *Batman Gotham Adventures.* DC Comics Paper, 2000. ISBN: 1-56389-616-8. Gr. 5-10

Tolkien, J. R. R. *The Hobbit: An Illustrated Edition of the Fantasy Classic (Abridged).* Ballantine Books, 2001. ISBN: 0-613-53684-3. Gr. 5-8

Vaughn, Brian K. *The Last Man: Unmanned.* Vertigo/DC Comics, 2003. ISBN: 1-56389-980-9. Gr. 10 & up. Adult

Waid, Mark. *Ruse: Inferno of Blue.* Cross Generation Paper, 2002. ISBN: 1-931484-19-8. Gr. 7-12

Warner, Allen. *Ninja Boy: Faded Dreams, 2003.* DC Comics Paper, 2003. ISBN: 1-4012-0102-4. Gr. 8-12

Watterson, Richard. *Calvin and Hobbes.* Andrews McMeel Publishing, 1987. ISBN: 0-8362-2088-9. Adult

Winick, Judd. *Pedro and Me: Friendship, Loss, and What I Learned.* Holt, 2000. ISBN: 0-8050-6403-6. Gr. 8-12

Annotated Journal Article

Foster, Katy. "Graphic Novels in Libraries: An Expert's Opinion." *Library Media Connection* **(February 2004): 30-32.**

This article is written as if Barbara Gordon, librarian and computer expert from Gotham City and the property of DC Comics, were the author. She is pleading the case of graphic novels in the library. She states that there are six basic types of graphic novels and that these novels are useful in getting reluctant readers to read because they are fun and current. She claims that readers can be taught all the standard lessons on plot, conflict, setting, flashbacks, foreshadowing, etc., using graphic novels and that males are often the heroes—enticing boys to read their stories.

11

Realistic Fiction

Introduction

It is comforting to know that we are not alone when we experience upsets and dilemmas. Boys can strengthen character and develop understanding of peers, teachers, parents, and siblings by reading realistic stories set in recent times. Seeing how others deal with issues and realizing that they, too, will overcome their problems helps boys to be more understanding and feel better about themselves.

Discussion Questions

- Did you learn anything about yourself when reading this book?

- Have you been in a similar situation?

- How did the main character handle the issues presented in this book?

- Do you know anyone who is like the main character?

- How would this story have changed if the main character did things differently or made different choices?

- How important is it to seek help when things are getting rough?

- Do you know an adult who will help you if you ask?

Annotations

Clements, Andrew. *A Week in the Woods.* **Simon & Schuster, 2004. ISBN: 0-689-85802-7. Gr. 4-6**

Mark was a new student in a small public school. He knew he would be going to a boarding school next year, so in the meantime he kept his distance from the other students. When Mr. Maxwell announces the environmental camping trip, Mark comes around and signs up for the trip. On the first day of the trip, Mr. Maxwell finds a tool on Mark that contains a knife, which was not allowed. He punishes Mark by attempting to send him home, but Mark runs away. Mr. Maxwell, still out to teach Mark a lesson, follows him with the hope that he can rescue Mark. It turns out that Mr. Maxwell sprains his ankle and Mark is a prepared camper. Together they make it back to camp.

Cooney, Caroline B. *Driver's Ed.* **Delacorte, 1994. ISBN: 0-385-32087-6. YA**

Remy and Morgan accept a class challenge to steal highway signs. Along with Nickie, who is driving, they steal *THICKLY SETTLED, MORGAN ROAD,* and finally a *STOP* sign. Remy and Morgan are more concerned with each other than what they just did, until later that night a young mother dies in a tragic car accident at the same corner where they had stolen the stop sign. The woman's husband appears on television and offers a reward to anyone with information about the vandalism that led to his wife's death.

Cormier, Robert. *The Chocolate War.* **Pantheon Books, 1974. ISBN: 0-394-82805-4. Gr. 6 & up**

Jerry has a poster of a solitary man standing upright on the beach, mounted inside his locker. Inscribed on the poster is the slogan: "Do I Dare Disturb the Universe." Jerry comes to understand the poster when he defies a teacher; the Vigils, an underground organization; and ultimately the entire school. He sadly learns that people only let you do your own thing when it happens to be their own thing.

———. *The Rag and Bone Shop.* **Delacorte, 2001. ISBN: 0-385-72962-6. Gr. 7 & up**

Twelve-year-old Jason was the last to see his seven-year-old neighbor alive. She was brutally murdered, her body found in the woods covered with leaves. It is a high-profile case; there is no evidence, but the police call in a well-known interrogator named Trent, who always gets a confession. When Jason meets Trent he thinks he is helping. His father is away on a business trip and his mother lets him go off with the police, assuring him that he has a duty to assist. The end results are devastating for both Trent and Jason.

Creech, Sharon. *Love That Dog.* **HarperCollins Children's Book Group, 2001. ISBN: 0-06-029287-3. Gr. 3-6**

Through poetry, the story gradually unfolds of a young boy and his yellow dog, Sky, who chases a ball into the street and is hit by a car and dies. Initially the student resists poetry but eventually uses many famous poems and the inspiration of the poet, Walter Dean Myers, to help him write his own poem about Sky.

Draper, Sharon M. *The Battle of Jericho.* **Atheneum, 2003. ISBN: 0-689-84232-5. YA**

Jericho has always felt on the outside of things at his high school in spite of his musical abilities. He has an opportunity to join an unofficial school-sponsored club, Warriors of Distinction. First he must pass a series of humiliations and engage activities that are suppose to create bonding, unity, strength, and power among the members. But at what point do these initiations cross the line and become harassment and hazing? Could this club be good and bad at the same time? Jericho is becoming more and more uneasy. When it is all over Jericho will not be the same for a long, long time.

Koertge, Ronald. *Stoner & Spaz.* **Candlewick Press, 2002. ISBN: 0-7636-1608-7. Gr. 8-12**

Sixteen-year-old Ben Bancroft has cerebral palsy, no parents, and a wealthy, overprotective grandmother. He is a loner who is addicted to old movies. Colleen Minou is always high, her clothes are from the Salvation Army, she is tattooed everywhere, and she has a foul mouth. The two become a couple. She is the first one who ever really noticed Ben and who actually teases him about his disability. She takes him to clubs, gives him his first joint, and challenges him to direct his own movie. He challenges her to get off the drugs—but she is unable to do so. What will happen to Ben, who is seriously addicted to Colleen?

Koja, Kathe. *Buddha Boy.* **Farrar, Straus & Giroux, 2003. ISBN: 0-374-30998-1. Gr. 7 & up**

No matter what they did to Jinsen, he smiled or ignored his tormentors, as if to say "keep trying 'til they (get) got it right." Justin gradually befriends Jinsen, at the risk of himself being targeted. Their friendship develops over their mutual love of art. Jinsen is working on a large banner with hopes of getting a summer internship with the Creative Art Center. Before he is able to bring the banner to the CAC as part of a portfolio, the bullies strike again. This time is it Justin who is able to calm Jinsen before he reverts to the way he used to be, a bully just like his tormentors.

Lester, Julius. *When Dad Killed Mom.* **Harcourt Paper, 2003. ISBN: 0-15-204698-4. YA**

The lives of Jenna and Jeremy are changed forever when their dad kills their mom. Clearly their parents' marriage was in trouble, but neither child thought their father was capable of such violence. This story follows the changes and emotions of both children, from that day when they were pulled from their classrooms and told what happened until the day after the trial, when the children decide who is going to be responsible for them. A gripping, emotional novel of loss and growth.

Levithan, David. *Boy Meets Boy.* **Alfred A. Knopf, 2003. ISBN: 0-375-92400-0. YA**

From an early age Paul has known that he is gay. When he was in the third grade he ran for the president of his class as a gay president. His other friends have not been as lucky. Tony has to keep his true identity a secret because of the religious convictions of his parents. Kyle is lost and has feelings for both boys and girls. This book is about Paul's relationship with each of his individual friends, including Joni, but in particular Noah, who is new to the school. Paul makes some mistakes, but he bravely shows how he feels to his friends and especially Noah.

Lubar, David. *Dunk.* **Clarion, 2002. ISBN: 0-618-19455-X. Gr. 7-10**

Chad lives near the Jersey shore and has always been fascinated by the dunk tank at the amusement park every summer. He wants to get a job as the Bozo or the one who is inside the cage suspended over the tank. Chad's father ran out on him and his mom, and everyone thinks that Chad will become a loser, too.

Myers, Walter Dean. *145th Street Short Stories.* **Delacorte, 2000. ISBN: 0-385-32137-6. Gr. 7-12**

Life on 145th Street in Harlem is hard, and you have to take it seriously. These 10 stories all take place on 145th Street. They include "Big Joe's Funeral," "A Christmas Story," "Monkeyman," and "Block Party—145th Street Style."

Park, Barbara. *The Graduation of Jake Moon.* **Simon & Schuster, 2002. ISBN: 0-689-839855. Gr.4-6**

Jake and two eighth-grade friends are on the way home from school when they begin to make fun of an old man in a dumpster. Jake lets it happen and doesn't let on that the old man is his grandfather, Skelly. Jake has always been very close to his grandfather but he doesn't know how to handle Skelly's Alzheimer's disease. As Jake reminisces about Skelly his guilt lessens, and he reconciles with Skelly. Jake is forced to publicly acknowledge and rescue his grandfather during his eighth-grade graduation.

Smith, Roland. *Zach's Lie.* **Hyperion, 2001. ISBN: 0-7868-0617-6. Gr. 5-9**

Jack Osborne, along with his mother and sister, enter the witness protection program after they are threatened by drug dealers. Jack becomes Zach Granger, and they begin a new life in a small town. Zach knows that their lives may have been spared but feels that reality is "lives" missing the letter V.

Spinelli, Jerry. *Wringer.* **HarperCollins, 1977. ISBN: 0-06-024913-7. Gr. 3-7**

Palmer LaRue received the treatment when he was nine. It consisted of nine hard ones by a knuckle on his left arm along with a new name, Snots. The treatment was part of the town's tradition, along with Family Fest in August. The festival was a week of bumper cars, music, and cotton candy. It culminated on Saturday with Pigeon Day. On Pigeon Day, crates and crates of pigeons were brought into town. As the pigeons were released, the shooters took aim and fired. Those pigeons that were wounded or flopping around were put out of their misery by wringers. Palmer dreaded his 10th birthday because then he, too, could be a wringer. Would he have the courage to oppose tradition and his friends' expectations?

Strasser, Todd. *Give a Boy a Gun.* **Simon & Schuster, 2000. ISBN: 0-689-81112-8. Gr. 7-12**

Two boys, Gary Searle and Brendan Lawlor, hold students hostage in a gym with automatic weapons and homemade bombs. Denise Shipley, Gary's stepsister, arrives home after the tragedy to interview friends, neighbors, teachers, and students to try to find out how and why this happened. Additional facts and statistics about guns and their usage are found throughout, set apart by a dotted line and smaller type. The author states in the Author's Note, "The story you are about to read is a work of fiction. Nothing—and everything—about it is real."

Van Draanen, Wendelin. *Swear to Howdy.* **Alfred A. Knopf, 2003. ISBN: 0-375-82505-3. Gr. 5-7**

Rusty and Joey are next door neighbors who constantly make pacts to maintain each other's trust. In many ways their families are alike, except when Joey's father is drinking. Joey is always thinking up a prank or a new adventure. One night they sneak out with materials to create the Lost Ghost of the River. Several cars go over the bridge, and the boys flutter the ghost without incident. Then a car loses control when Joey flutters the ghost. The car belongs to Joey's older sister, and she dies in the crash that follows. Now Joey and Rusty once again swear not to tell a soul, no matter what happens.

Werlin, Nancy. *The Killer's Cousin.* **Bantam Books, 1998. ISBN: 0-385-32560-6. Gr. 9-12**

David has just been acquitted of killing his girlfriend, and his family is sending him to live with his aunt and uncle and 11-year-old Lily. David will repeat his senior year of high school and hopes to get his life back in order. Lily is intent on harassing and tormenting David. Why is she doing this? Why won't anyone believe David when he says Lily needs help?

Woodson, Jacqueline. *Locomotion*. Penguin Group, 2003. ISBN: 0-399-23115-3. Gr. 4-6
    Lonnie Collins Motion was called "locomotion" after the song, "Lo Co Motion." With help and encouragement from his teacher, he discovers a new way to put his feelings down on paper. He tells his story in the poems he writes about being in a group home; his younger sister, Lili; family memories; and Miss Edna, his new foster mom. When he was seven, Lonnie's parents were killed in a fire, and after being passed around among relatives who didn't have room, he was placed in foster care and separated from Lili. Lonnie manages a way to see his sister on a regular basis and finds a bigger brother when Miss Edna's son comes to live with them.

Bibliography

Atinsky, Steve. *Tyler on Prime Time*. Delacorte, 2002. ISBN: 0-385-72917-8. Gr. 5-7

Atkins, Catherine. *Alt Ed*. Putnam, 2003. ISBN: 0-399-23854-9. Gr. 7-10

Avi. *Nothing but the Truth: A Documentary Novel*. Orchard, 1991. ISBN: 0-531-08559-7. Gr. 7-10

Bauer, Marion Dane. *On My Honor*. Houghton, 1986. ISBN: 0-89919-439-7. Gr. 5-7

Bloor, Edward. *Tangerine*. Harcourt, 1997. ISBN: 0-15-201246-X. Gr. 7-10

Bruchac, Joseph. *Heart of a Chief*. Dial, 1998. ISBN: 0-8037-2276-1. Gr. 5-8

Carlson, Ron. *The Speed of Light*. HarperTempest, 2003. ISBN: 0-380-97837-7. Gr. 4-7

Cart, Michael, ed. *Love and Sex*. Simon & Schuster, 2003. ISBN: 0-689-85668-7. YA Mature

Carvell, Marlene. *Who Will Tell My Brother?* Hyperion, 2002. ISBN: 0-7868-0827-6. Gr. 7-12

Chbosky, Stephen. *The Perks of Being a Wallflower*. Simon & Schuster, 1999. ISBN: 0-671- 02734-4. Gr. 7-12

Clements, Andrew. *The Janitor's Boy*. Simon & Schuster, 2001. ISBN: 0-689-83585-X. Gr. 3-7

Crutcher, Chris. *Staying Fat for Sarah Brynes*. Greenwillow, 1993. ISBN: 0-688-11552-7. Gr. 7-12

Danticat, Edwidge. *Behind the Mountains*. Scholastic, 2002. ISBN: 0-430-37299-2. Gr. 5-8

Danziger, Paula. *United Tates of America*. Scholastic, 2002. ISBN: 0-590-69221-6. Gr. 3-7

Divakaruni, Chitra Banerjee. *The Conch Bearer*. Roaring Brook, 2004. ISBN: 0-7613-1935-2. Gr. 5-9

Donahue, John. *Till Tomorrow*. Farrar, Straus & Giroux, 2001. ISBN: 0-374-37580-1. Gr. 5-7

Duffey, Betsy. *Fur-Ever Yours, Booker Jones*. Penguin, 2001. ISBN: 0-670-89287-4. Gr. 4-6

Farrell, Mame. *And Sometimes Why*. Farrar, Straus & Giroux, 2001. ISBN: 0-374-32289-9. Gr. 6-9

Fine, Anne. *Up on Cloud Nine*. Delacorte, 2002. ISBN: 0-385-73009-8. Gr. 5-8

Fleischman, Paul. *Seek*. Cricket, 2001. ISBN: 0-8126-4900-1. Gr. 7-12

Fogelin, Adrian. *Crossing Jordan.* Peachtree, 2000. ISBN: 1-56145-215-7. Gr. 5-8

Gantos, Jack. *Jack Adrift: Fourth Grade Without a Clue.* Farrar, Straus & Giroux, 2003. ISBN: 0-374-39987-5. Gr. 4-6

————. *Joey Pigza Loses Control.* Farrar, Straus & Giroux, 2000. ISBN: 0-374-39989-1. Gr. 4-7.

————. *Joey Pigza Swallowed the Key.* Farrar, Straus & Giroux, 1998. ISBN: 0-374-33664-4. Gr. 4-8

Gilbert, Barbara Snow. *Paper Trail.* Front Street, 2000. ISBN: 1-886910-44-8. Gr. 7-10

Grimes, Nikki. *Bronx Masquerade.* Dial, 2002. ISBN: 0-8037-2569-9. Gr. 7-12

Hartinger, Bret. *Geography Club.* HarperCollins, 2003. ISBN: 0-06-001221-8. Gr. 9-12

Holt, Kimberly Willis. *When Zachary Beaver Came to Town.* Holt, 1999. ISBN: 0-8050-6116-9. Gr. 5-9

Holtwijk, Ineke. *Asphalt Angels.* Front Street, 1999. ISBN: 1-886910-24-3. Gr. 8-12 YA Mature

Huser, Glen. *Stitches.* Groundwood, 2004. ISBN: 0-88899-553-9. Gr. 4-6

Jenkins, A. M. *Damage.* HarperCollins, 2001. ISBN: 0-06-029099-4. Gr. 7 & up

————. *Out of Order.* HarperCollins, 2003. ISBN: 0-06-623968-0. Gr. 8-10

Johnston, Tony. *Any Small Goodness: A Novel of the Barrio.* Scholastic, 2001. ISBN: 0-439-18936-5. Gr. 4-7

Korman, Gordan. *Jake, Reinvented.* Hyperion, 2003. ISBN: 0-7868-1957-X. YA

Lester, Julius. *Long Journey Home.* Viking Paper, 1998. ISBN: 0-14-038981-4. Gr. 6-8

MacDonald, Amy. *No More Nasty.* Farrar, Straus & Giroux, 2001. ISBN: 0-374-35529-0. Gr. 3-7

Martin, Nora. *A Perfect Snow.* Bloomsbury, 2002. ISBN: 1-58234-788-3. Gr. 7-10

Martinez, Victor. *Parrot in the Oven: Mi Vida.* HarperCollins, 1996. ISBN: 0-06-026706-2. Gr. 7-10

McNamee, Graham. *Sparks.* Random, 2002. ISBN: 0-385-72977-4. Gr. 3-5

Mochizuki, Ken. *Beacon Hill Boys.* Scholastic, 2002. ISBN: 0-439-26749-8. Gr. 7-10

Myers, Walter Dean. *The Beast.* Scholastic, 2003. ISBN: 0-439-36841-3. YA

————. *The Dream Bearer.* HarperCollins, 2003. ISBN: 0-06-029521-X. Gr. 5-8

————. *Monster.* HarperCollins, 1999. ISBN: 0-06-028077-8. YA

Nolan, Han. *When We Were Saints.* Harcourt, 2003. ISBN: 0-15-216371-9. Gr. 7-10

Paulsen, Gary. *The Glass Café.* Random, 2003. ISBN: 0-385-32499-5. Gr. 6-8

Philbrick, Rodman. *Freak the Mighty.* Scholastic, 1993. ISBN: 0-590-47412-X. Gr. 7-10

Ranulfo. *Nirvana's Children.* HarperCollins, 2003. ISBN: 0-06-054155-5. YA

Rottman, S.L. *Shadow of a Doubt.* Peachtree Publishers, 2003. ISBN: 1-561-45291-2. Gr. 7 & up

Saldana, Rene, Jr. *The Jumping Tree: A Novel.* Delacorte, 2001. ISBN: 0-385-32725-0. Gr. 5-9

Sanchez, Alex. *Rainbow High.* Simon & Schuster, 2003. ISBN: 0-689-85477-3. YA Mature

Seidler, Tor. *The Dulcimer Boy.* HarperCollins, 2003. ISBN: 0-06-023609-6. Gr. 4-8

Soto, Gary. *Petty Crimes.* Harcourt, 1998. ISBN: 0-15-201658-9. Gr. 5-8

Springer, Nancy. *Blood Trail.* Holiday, 2003. ISBN: 0-8234-1723-8. Gr. 6-8

Tashjian, Janet. *Fault Line.* Holt, 2003. ISBN: 0-8050-7200-4. YA

———. *The Gospel According to Larry.* Holt, 2001. ISBN: 0-8050-6378-1. Gr. 7-10

Thomas, Rob. *Doing Time: Notes from the Undergrad.* Simon & Schuster, 1997. ISBN: 0-689-80958-1. Gr. 8-10

———. *Rats Saw God.* Simon & Schuster, 1996. ISBN: 0-689-80777-5. Gr. 8-12

Van Draanen, Wendelin. *Flipped.* Knopf, 2001. ISBN: 0-375-81174-5. Gr. 5-8

Wilhelm, Doug. *Raising the Shades.* Farrar, Straus & Giroux, 2001. ISBN: 0-374-36178-9. Gr. 6-8

Williams-Garcia, Rita. *Every Time a Rainbow Dies.* HarperCollins, 2001. ISBN: 0-06-029202-4. Gr. 5 & up

Wilson, Jacqueline. *The Worry Web Site.* Delacorte, 2003. ISBN: 0-385-73083-7. Gr. 3-7

Wittinger, Ellen. *Hard Love.* Simon & Schuster, 1999. ISBN: 0-689-82134-4. Gr. 8-12

———. *Razzle.* Simon & Schuster, 2001. ISBN: 0-689-83565-5. Gr. 7-12

Wynne-Jones, Tim. *Lord of the Fries and Other Stories.* DK Paper, 1999. ISBN: 0-7894-2623-4. Gr. 6-10

Yep, Laurence. *Dragonwings.* HarperCollins, 1975. ISBN: 0-06-026738-0. Gr. 7-9

Nonfiction

Bode, Janet, and Stan Mack. *Heartbreak and Roses: Real Life Stories of Troubled Love.* Scholastic, 2000. ISBN: 0-531-16464-0. YA

———. *Trust and Betrayal: Real Life Stories of Friends and Enemies.* Delacorte, 1996. ISBN: 0-385-30990-2. Juv

Gallo, Donald R., ed. *No Easy Answers: Short Stories about Teenagers Making Tough Choices.* Delacorte, 1997. ISBN: 0-385-32290-9. Gr. 6-12

Haskins, Pearl Fuyo. *What Are You? Voices of Mixed-Race Young People.* Holt, 1999. ISBN: 0-8050-5968-7. Gr. 7-12

Hopkinson, Deborah. *Shutting Out the Sky: Life in the Tenements of New York, 1880–1924.* Scholastic, 2003. ISBN: 0-439-37590-8. Juv

Lewis, J. Patrick. *The Last Resort.* Creative Company, 2002. ISBN: 1-56846-172-0. Gr. 6-9

Mastoon, Adam. *The Shared Heart: Portraits and Stories Celebrating Lesbian, Gay, and Bisexual Young People.* Morrow, 1997. ISBN: 0-688-14931-6. YA Mature

Mazer, Harry, ed. *Twelve Shots: Outstanding Short Stories about Guns.* Delacorte, 1997. ISBN: 0-385-44698-5. Adult

Morris, Deborah. *Teens 911: Snowbound Helicopter Crash and Other True Survival Stories.* Health Communications Paper, 2002. ISBN: 0-7573-0039-1. Gr. 7-12

Muse, Daphne, ed. *Prejudice: Stories about Hate, Ignorance, Revelation, and Transformation.* Hyperion, 1995. ISBN: 0-606-15684-4. Juv

Son, John. *Finding My Hat.* Scholastic, 2003. ISBN: 0-439-43538-2. Gr. 4-8

Yep, Laurence, ed. *American Dragons: Twenty-Five Asian American Voices.* HarperCollins, 1995. ISBN: 0-06-440603-2. Gr. 7-12

Picture Books

Bunting, Eve. *Fly Away Home.* Clarion, 1991. ISBN: 0-395-55962-6. Juv

———. *Smoky Night.* Harcourt, 1994. ISBN: 0-15-269954-6. Juv

Carrick, Carol. *Whaling Days.* Houghton Mifflin, 1993. ISBN: 0-395-50948-3. Juv

Fox, Mem. *Wilfrid Gordon McDonald Partridge.* Kane/Miller, 1989. ISBN: 0-916291-26-X. Juv

Gaiman, Neil. *The Wolves in the Walls.* HarperCollins, 2003. ISBN: 0-380-97827-X. Gr. 1 & up

Johnson, Stephen T. *As the City Sleeps.* Viking, 2002. ISBN: 0-670-88940-7. Juv

Rodriguez, Luis J. *It Doesn't Have to Be This Way: A Barrio Story.* Children's Book Press, 1999. ISBN: 0-89239-161-8. Juv

Rylant, Cynthia. *An Angel for Solomon Singer.* Scholastic, 1996. ISBN: 0-531-07082-4. Juv

Say, Allen. *Grandfather's Journey.* Houghton, 1993. ISBN: 0-395-57035-2. Juv

Taylor, Clark. *The House That Crack Built.* Chronicle, 1992. ISBN: 0-8118-0123-3. Juv

Annotated Journal Articles

Crutcher, Chris. "The Outsiders: If Columbine and Similar Tragedies Have Taught Us Anything about Teens, It Is the Value of Belonging and the Dangers of Isolation." *School Library Journal* **(August 2001): 54-56.**

Crutcher reminds us that we often fail to remember that adolescence is a developmental stage in which teens are pushing away and moving toward adulthood. We should not judge teens too harshly, and we should not take their actions personally. No teen wants to be lonely, all teens want to belong, and those outsiders should not be feared as potential "shooters" but should instead be invited in to become a part of a group or community. What better place to belong than in a classroom or a school library?

Scales, Pat. "The Pigman and He." *School Library Journal* (June 2002): 53-54.

Paul Zindel states that all teens are full of fear and self-loathing, and they each desperately need an unconditional friend like the pigman. He says that parents today are too busy with their own lives to be very supportive of their teens and that having an important and trustworthy adult friend to depend on would be a tremendous help to teens today.

Appendix A

Author Information Just for Boys

Author: Avi (Michael Avi-Yonah)
>Birthplace: Brooklyn, New York
>Date of Birth: December 27, 1937
>Current Home: Providence, Rhode Island

Titles:

No More Magic (1975)
Captain Grey (1977)
Sometimes I Think I Hear My Name (1982)
The Fighting Ground (1984)
Romeo & Juliet, Together and Alive at Last (1987)
Something Upstairs (1988)
The Man Who Was Poe (1989)
The True Confessions of Charlotte Doyle (1990)
Windcatcher (1991)
Nothing But the Truth: A Documentary Novel (1991)
Who Was that Masked Man Anyway? (1992)
Blue Heron (1993)
City of Light, City of Dark: A Comic Book Novel (1993)
Man from the Sky (1994)
Bright Shadow (1994)
The Barn (1994)
Night Journeys (1994)
Poppy (1995)
Beyond the Western Sea: The Escape from Home (1996)
Beyond the Western Sea: Lord Kirkle's Money (1996)
Poppy & Rye (1998)
Who Stole the Wizard of Oz? (1999)
Devil's Race (1999)
Midnight Magic (1999)
A Place Called Ugly (1999)
Perloo the Bold (1999)
Smuggler's Island (1999)

Ragweed: Tales from Dimwood Forest (1999)
Wolf Rider (2000)
Encounter at Easton (2000)
S.O.R Losers (2000)
The Christmas Rat (2000)
Ereth's Birthday: Tales from Dimwood Forest (2000)
The Secret School (2001)
The Good Dog (2001)
Don't You Know There's a War On? (2001)
Crispin: The Cross of Lead (2002)
Silent Movie (2003)

Interesting Information:

He got the nickname Avi from his sister.
He has a learning disability that makes writing by hand difficult.
Avi says the key to good writing is reading.

Web Site: http://www.avi-writer.com

Contact:

c/o HarperCollins
1350 Avenue of the Americas
New York, NY 10019

Author: Joseph Bruchac

Birthplace: Saratoga Springs, New York
Date of Birth: 1942
Current Home: Greenfield Center, New York

Titles:

Keepers of the Animals (1991)
Thirteen Moons on a Turtle's Back: A Native American Year of Moons (1992)
Dog People: Native American Stories (1995)
Children of the Longhouse (1996)
Eagle Song (1997)
Tell Me a Tale (1997)
Keepers of Life (1997)
When the Chenoo Howls (1998)
The Heart of a Chief (1998)
The Arrow Over the Door (1998)
Pushing Up the Sky (2000)
Skeleton Man (2001)
The Journal of Jesse Smoke (2001)
Bowman's Store (2001)
Navajo Long Walk (2002)
The Winter People (2002)
Native American Animal Stories (Myths and Legends) (2003)
Our Stories Remember (2003)
The Warriors (2003)
The Dark Pond (2004)
Hidden Roots (2004)
A Code Talker's Story (2005)

Interesting Information:
He was raised by his grandparents and has been an avid reader from childhood.
He plays guitar, flute, and drum;—he sometimes plays songs he writes.
Bruchac says we must learn to listen to each other and to the earth.
Web Site: http://www.josephbruchac.com
Contact:
P.O. Box 308
Greenfield Center, NY 12833
Phone: (518) 584-1728
Fax: (518) 583-9741
E-mail: nudatlog@earthlink.net

Author: Bruce Coville
Birthplace: Syracuse, New York
Date of Birth: May 16, 1950
Current Home: Syracuse, New York
Titles:
William Shakespeare's Macbeth (1987)
The Ghost Wore Gray (1988)
The Ghost in the Big Brass Bed (1991)
Goblins in the Castle (1992)
My Teacher Flunked the Planet (1992)
Space Brat (1993)
Aliens Ate My Homework (1993)
I Left My Sneakers in Dimension X (1994)
The Dragonslayers (1994)
The Wrath of Squat (1994)
The Search for Snout (1995)
The Planet of the Dips (1995)
Bruce Coville's Book of Nightmares (1995)
William Shakespeare's a Midsummer Night's Dream (1996)
Is Your Teacher an Alien? (1997)
The Worlds Worst Fairy Godmother (1997)
Oddly Enough (1997)
Armageddon Summer (with Jane Yolen) (1998)
My Teacher Is an Alien (1999)
The Ghost in the Third Row (1999)
My Teacher Fried My Brains (1999)
My Teacher Glows in the Dark (1999)
Into the Land of the Unicorns (1999)
Aliens Stole My Body (1999)
Bruce Coville's Shape Shifters (1999)
Song of the Wanderer (1999)
I Was a Sixth Grade Alien (1999)
I Lost My Grandfathers Brain (1999)
The Attack of the Two-Inch Teacher (2000)
A Glory of Unicorns (2000)
Snatched from Earth (2000)

Peanut Butter Lover Boy (2000)
Zombies of the Science Fair (2000)
Dont Fry My Veeblax! (2000)
Odder Than Ever (2000)
Too Many Aliens (2000)
Theres an Alien in My Backpack (2000)
Bruce Coville's UFOs (2000)
The Revolt of the Miniature Mutants (2001)
Theres an Alien in My Underware (2001)
Farewell to Earth (2001)
The Monsters of Morley Manor (2001)
Half-Human (2001)
Jeremy Thatcher, Dragon Hatcher (2002)
The Skull of Truth (2002)
The Monsters Ring (2002)
The Dragon of Doom (Moongobble and Me) (2003)
William Shakespeare's Twelfth Night (2003)
William Shakespeare's Hamlet (2004)
The Weeping Werewolf (Moongobble and Me) (2004)
The Evil Elves (Moongobble and Me) (2004)
The Unicorn Treasury (2004)

Interesting Information:

He wanted to be a writer since sixth grade.

He has written musical plays, contributed to anthologies of fantasy stories, and written picture books.

He is fascinated by myths and mythical imagery.

Web Site: http://www.brucecoville.com/

Contact:

Oddly Enough
P.O. Box 6110
Syracuse, NY 13217

Author: Chris Crutcher

Birthplace: Dayton, Ohio
Date of Birth: July 17, 1946
Current Home: Spokane, Washington

Titles:

Running Loose (1983)
Stotan! (1986)
Chinese Handcuffs (1989)
Athletic Shorts (1991)
Staying Fat for Sarah Byrnes (1993)
Ironman (1995)
Whale Talk (2001)
The Crazy Horse Electric Game (2003)
King of the Mild Frontier: An Ill-Advised Autobiography (2003)

Interesting Information:

He did not like to read as a child.

He was an excellent swimmer and runner.

He became a child and family therapist.

Web Site: http://www.aboutcrutcher.com/

Contact:

Chris PREFERS e-mail, so please contact him at Stotan717@aol.com

Letters:

c/o HarperCollins/Greenwillow

1350 Avenue of the Americas

New York, NY 10019-4703

Or contact his publicist at: josette.kurey@harpercollins.com

Author: Carl Deuker

Birthplace: San Francisco, California

Date of Birth: August 26, 1950

Current Home: Seattle, Washington

Titles:

On the Devil's Court (1988)

Heart of a Champion (1993)

Painting the Black (1997)

Night Hoops (2000)

Interesting Information:

He writes books about good kids who sometimes do foolish things.

He is a teacher and writes before and sometime after work.

He has a pet guinea pig.

Web Site: http://members.authorsguild.net/carldeuker/bio.htm

Contact:

E-mail: carl1989@hotmail.com

Author: Russell Freedman

Birthplace: San Francisco, California

Date of Birth: October 11, 1929

Current Home: New York, New York

Titles:

Children of the Wild West (1983)

Buffalo Hunt (1988)

Lincoln: A Photobiography (1989)

Franklin Delano Roosevelt (1990)

Indian Chiefs (1992)

Eleanor Roosevelt: A Life of Discovery (1993)

The Wright Brothers: How They Invented the Airplane (1994)

Kids at Work: Lewis Hine and the Crusade Against Child Labor (1994)

Immigrant Kids (1995)

Out of Darkness: The Story of Louis Braille (1997)

Babe Didrikson Zaharias: The Making of a Champion (1999)

Give Me Liberty!: The Story of the Declaration of Independence (2000)

In the Days of the Vaqueros: America's First True Cowboys (2001)

Confucius: The Golden Rule (2002)

In Defense of Liberty: The Story of America's Bill of Rights (2003)

The Voice That Challenged a Nation: Marian Anderson and the Struggle for Equal Rights (2004)

Interesting Information:

His father was a publishing rep for Macmillan, so famous authors often came to dinner at his house.

His favorite books as a child were *Treasure Island* and *Wild Animals I Have Known.*

His interest in wild animals continued into nonfiction in general.

Web Site: N/A

Contact:

c/o Clarion Books

215 Park Avenue South

New York, NY 10003

Author: Jack Gantos

Birthplace: Mt. Pleasant, Pennsylvania

Date of Birth: July 2, 1951

Current Home: Boston, Massachusetts

Titles:

Joey Pigza Swallowed the Key (1998)

Joey Pigza Loses Control (2000)

What Would Joey Do? (2002)

Hole in My Life (2002)

Interesting Information:

He has been writing since he was in sixth grade.

His stories are based on his life—he really did have a cat exactly like Rotten Ralph!

Hole in My Life is his prison memoir—he actually did time in prison.

Web Site: http://www.jackgantos.com

Contact:

c/o Children's Marketing Department

Farrar Straus Giroux Books for Young Readers

19 Union Square West

New York, NY 10003

Author: Margaret Peterson Haddix

Birthplace: Washington Court House, Ohio

Date of Birth: 1964

Current Home: Columbus, Ohio

Titles:

Running Out of Time (1995)

Don't You Dare Read This, Mrs. Dunphrey (1996)

Leaving Fishers (1997)

Among the Hidden (1998)

Just Ella (1999)

Turnabout (2000)

Among the Imposters (2001)

Takeoffs and Landings (2001)

The Girl with 500 Middle Names (2001)

Among the Betrayed (2002)

Because of Anya (2002)

Anya's Wig (2002)

Escape from Memory (2003)
Among the Barons (2003)
Say What? (2004)
Among the Brave (2004)
Shadow Children (2004)
The House on the Gulf (2004)
Interesting Information:
She had a short attention span during most of her childhood.
She spent much of her time reading and writing in secret.
Her ideas come from past experiences.
Web Site: N/A
Contact:
c/o Simon & Schuster Books for Young Readers
1230 Avenue of the Americas
New York, NY 10020

Author: S. E. Hinton (Susan Eloise Hinton)
Birthplace: Tulsa, Oklahoma
Date of Birth: 1950
Current Home: Tulsa, Oklahoma
Titles:
The Outsiders (1967)
That Was Then, This Is Now (1971)
Rumble Fish (1975)
Tex (1989)
Taming the Star Runner (1999)
Hawkes Harbor (2004)
Interesting Information:
As a child she was a tomboy who loved horses.
She reads everything—all the time!
Royalties from *The Outsiders* helped her finance her education at University of Tulsa.
Web Site: http://www.sehinton.com
Contact:
E-mail: sehinton@sehinton.com

Author: Will Hobbs
Birthplace: Pittsburgh, Pennsylvania
Date of Birth: August 22, 1947
Current Home: Durango, Colorado
Titles:
Bearstone (1989)
The Big Wander (1992)
Beardance (1993)
Kokopelli's Flute (1995)
Far North (1996)
Ghost Canoe (1997)
River Thunder (1997)
Beardream (1997)

The Maze (1998)
Howling Hill (1998)
Jason's Gold (1999)
Down the Yukon (2001)
Wild Man Island (2002)
Jackie's Wild Seattle (2003)
Leaving Protection (2004)

Interesting Information:

Will was a reading teacher for many years before becoming a writer.

Will liked everything to do with the outdoors.

Ideas for his books come from his own experiences.

Web Site: http://www.willhobbsauthor.com

Contact:

5 Sunridge Circle
Durango, CO 81301

Author: Brian Jacques

Birthplace: Liverpool, England
Date of Birth: June 15, 1939
Current Home: Liverpool, England

Titles:

Redwall (1987)
Mossflower (1988)
Seven Strange and Ghostly Tales (1991)
Mattimeo (1992)
Salamandastron (1993)
Martin the Warrior (1994)
The Bellmaker (1995)
Outcast of Redwall (1996)
The Pearls of Lutra (1997)
The Long Patrol (1998)
Redwall Map and the Redwall Riddler (1998)
Marlfox (1999)
The Legend of Luke (2000)
Lord Brocktree (2000)
Mariel of Redwall (2000)
Redwall Friend and Foe: The Guide to Redwall's Heroes and Villains (2000)
Taggerung (2001)
The Great Redwall Feast (2001)
A Redwall's Winter's Tale (2001)
Triss (2002)
Badgers (2002)
Loamhedge (2003)
Castaways of the Flying Dutchman (2003)
Otters (2003)
The Angel's Command (2003)
The Tribes of Redwall (2004)
The Ribbajack (2004)

Interesting Information:

His name is pronounced "jakes."

He started out as a seaman and traveled to many wonderful places.

He has been a fireman, a policeman, a truck driver, a bus driver, a boxer, and a comedian.

Web Site: http://www.redwall.org/

Contact:

Redwall Readers Club

P.O. Box 57

Mossley Hill

Liverpool, UK

L18 3NZ

Author: Gordon Korman

Birthplace: Montreal, Quebec, Canada

Date of Birth: October 23, 1963

Current Home: Toronto, New York, Florida

Titles:

This Can't Be Happening at Macdonald Hall (1978)

Go Jump in the Pool (1979)

Beware the Fish (1980)

I Want to Go Home (1981)

Who Is Bugs Potter (1980)

Our Man Weston (1982)

Bugs Potter LIVE at Nickaninny (1983)

The War with Mr. Wizzle (1982)

No Coins Please (1984)

Don't Care High (1985)

Son of Interflux (1986)

A Semester in the Life of a Garbage Bag (1987)

The Zucchini Warriors (1988)

Radio 5th Grade (1989)

Losing Joe's Place (1990)

Macdonald Hall Goes Hollywood (1991)

The D- Poems of Jeremy Bloom (1992)

The Twinkie Squad (1992)

The Toilet Paper Tigers (1993)

Why Did the Underwear Cross the Road (1994)

The Last-Place Sports Poems of Jeremy Bloom (1996)

Something Fishy at Macdonald Hall (1995)

The Chicken Doesn't Skate (1996)

Liar, Liar Pants on Fire (1997)

The Sixth Grade Nickname Game (1998)

No More Dead Dogs (1998)

Slapshots 1—The Stars from Mars (1999)

Nose Pickers from Outer Space (1999)

Slapshots 2— All-Mars All-Stars (1999)

The Toilet Paper Tigers (1999)

Planet of the Nose Pickers (2000)

Slapshots 3— The Face-off Phony (2000)
Your Mummy Is a Nose Picker (2000)
Slapshots 4—Cup Crazy (2000)
Invasion of the Nose Pickers (2001)
Shipwreck (Island Book 1) (2001)
Survival (Island Book 2) (2001)
Escape (Island Book 3) (2001)
The Jersey (2001)
Son of the Mob (2002)
The Contest (Everest Book 1) (2002)
The Climb (Everest Book 2) (2002)
The Summit (Everest Book 3) (2002)
Maxx Comedy: The Funniest Kid in America (2003)
Jake, Reinvented (2003)
Dive Trilogy (2003)

Interesting Information:

He writes out his stories first in long hand and then types them into the computer.
Fifty percent of what he writes really happened—the rest is imaginary.
He travels over 40,000 miles a year to promote his books and talk to kids.

Web Site: http://gordonkorman.com/

Contact:

c/o Scholastic Inc.
555 Broadway
New York NY 10012

Author: Julius Lester

Birthplace: St. Louis, Missouri
Date of Birth: January 27, 1939
Current Home: Amherst, Massachusetts

Titles:

To Be a Slave (1969)
Black Folktales (1969)
The Knee-High Man and Other Tales (1972)
Two Love Stories (1972)
The Last Tales of Uncle Remus (1994)
The Man Who Knew Too Much: A Moral Tale from the Baile of Zambia (1994)
Othello: A Novel (1995)
Sam and the Tigers: A New Telling of Little Black Sambo (1996)
When Dad Killed Mom (2001)

Interesting Information:

He was politically active in the early civil rights movement in the south—three of his great-grandparents had been slaves.
He became a musician and recorded two albums.
He was not a good writer in his younger years.

Web Site: N/A

Contact:

306 Old Springfield Road
Belchertown, MA 01007-9694
E-mail: lester@judnea.umass.edu

Author: David Lubar

Birthplace: Morristown, New Jersey
Date of Birth: March, 1955
Current Home: Pennsylvania

Titles:

The Psychozone (1997)
The Psychozone Kidzilla & Other Tales (1997)
Monster Road (1999)
Dunk (2002)
Hidden Talents (2003)
Flip (2003)
Wizards of the Game (2003)
In the Land of the Lawn Weenies and Other Misadventures (2003)
Dog Days (2004)

Interesting Information:

He loves to write about weird and fantastic creatures.
As a child and young adult he loved to read—mostly science fiction.
He has written many computer games for Nintendo and GameBoy.

Web Site: http://www.davidlubar.com

Contact:

E-mail: david@davidlubar.com

Author: Chris Lynch

Birthplace: Boston, Massachusetts
Date of Birth: July 2, 1962
Current Home: Ayrshire, Scotland

Titles:

Iceman (1994)
Gypsy Davey (1994)
Mick (1996)
Dog Eat Dog (1996)
Babes in the Woods (1997)
Johnny Chesthair (1997)
Scratch and the Sniffs (1997)
The Wolf Gang (1998)
Ladies' Choice (1999)
Shadow Boxer (1999)
Slot Machine (1999)
Whitechurch (1999)
Extreme Elvin (1999)
Gold Dust (2000)
All the Old Haunts (2001)
Freewill (2001)
Who the Man (2002)
The Gravedigger's Cottage (2004)

Interesting Information:

He writes honestly about things that interest teens and tries to make each novel new and different, and his books are often controversial.

He has Irish citizenship and lives in Scotland.

He has three brothers and three sisters, and he loves anything funny and loves to laugh.

Web Site: http://www.harperchildrens.com/authorintro/index.asp?authorid=12419

Contact:

c/o HarperCollins

1350 Avenue of the Americas

New York, NY 10019

Author: David Macaulay

Birthplace: England

Date of Birth: December 2, 1946

Current Home: Rhode Island

Titles:

The Way Things Work (1971)

Cathedral: The Story of Its Construction (1973)

City: A Story of Roman Planning and Construction (1974)

Pyramid (1975)

Castle (1977)

Great Moments in Architecture (1978)

Unbuilding (1980)

Mill (1983)

Baaa (1985)

Motel of the Mysteries (1988)

Ship (1993)

Rome Antics (1997)

The New Way Things Work (1998)

Building Big (2000)

Mosque (2003)

Interesting Information:

He works in a studio some distance away from his home.

At age 11 he moved with his family from England to New Jersey.

He graduated from Rhode Island School of Design and worked as an interior designer, a junior high school teacher, and a teacher at RISD.

Web Site: http://www.houghtonmifflinbooks.com/authors/macaulay/

Contact:

146 Water Street

Warren, RI 02885

Author: Walter Dean Myers

Birthplace: Martinsburg, West Virginia

Date of Birth: August 12, 1937

Current Home: Jersey City, New Jersey

Titles:

Won't Know Till I Get There (1982)

The Outside Shot (1984)

Adventure in Granada (1985)

The Hidden Shrine (1985)

Duel in the Desert (1986)

Ambush in the Amazon (1986)

Sweet Illusions (1987)

Crystal (1987)

Scorpions (1988)

Me, Mop, and the Moondance Kid (1988)

Fallen Angels (1988)

Fast Sam, Cool Clyde, and Stuff (1988)

The Young Landlords (1989)

The Mouse Rap (1990)

Now Is Your Time (1991)

Somewhere in the Darkness (1992)

Mop, Moondance, and the Nagasaki Knights (1992)

The Righteous Revenge of Artemis Bonner (1992)

Malcolm X: By Any Means Necessary (1993)

Young Martin's Promise 1993)

A Place Called Heartbreak: A Story of Vietnam (1993)

Brown Angels: An Album of Pictures and Verse (1993)

Dangerous Games (1993)

Darnell Rock Reporting (1994)

The Glory Field (1995)

The Story of the Three Kingdoms (1995)

Shadow of the Red Moon (1995)

Glorious Angels: An Album of Pictures and Verse (1995)

The Dragon Takes a Wife (1995)

Slam (1996)

Toussaint L'Ouverture (1996)

Smiffy Blue: Ace Crime Detective: The Case of the Missing Ruby and Other Stories (1996)

One More River to Cross: An African American Photograph Album (1996)

How Mr. Monkey Saw the Whole World (1996)

Harlem (1997)

Amistad: A Long Road to Freedom (1998)

Angel to Angel (1998)

Monster (1999)

At Her Majesty's Request (1999)

The Journal of Joshua Loper (1999)

The Journal of Scott Pendleton Collins: A World War II Soldier (1999)

145th Street Short Stories (2000)

Blues of Flats Brown (2000)

Bad Boy: A Memoir (2001)

The Greatest: Muhammad Ali (2001)

Patrol: An American Soldier in Vietnam (2001)

Journal of Biddy Owens, the Negro Leagues (2001)

The Beast (2003)

Shooter (2004)

Interesting Information:

His mother died when he was three and his father gave him up for adoption.

His adopted parents lived in Harlem, where he grew up.

As a child he had a speech impediment.
Web Site: http://www.walterdeanmyersbooks.com
Contact:

c/o HarperCollins
1350 Avenue of the Americas
New York, NY 10019

Author: Garth Nix

Birthplace: Melbourne, Australia
Date of Birth: 1963
Current Home: Sydney, Australia

Titles:

The Ragwitch (1990)
Sabriel (1995)
Shade's Children (1997)
The Fall (2000)
Castle (2000)
Aenir (2000)
Above the Veil (2001)
Into Battle (2001)
Lirael: Daughter of Clayr (2001)
The Violet Keystone (2001)
Abhorsen (2003)
Grim Tuesday (2004)
Mister Monday (2004)

Interesting Information:

Garth has traveled to many strange places around the world.
He spent five years as a part-time military man but did not like it.
He likes to find new, young authors and help them get published.

Web Site: http://www.garthnix.co.uk/
Contact:

E-mail: garthnix@ozemail.com.au

Author: Gary Paulsen

Birthplace: Minneapolis, Minnesota
Date of Birth: May 17, 1939
Current Home: New Mexico

Titles:

Tracker (1984)
The Crossing (1987)
The Island (1988)
The Voyage of the Frog (1989)
The Winter Room (1989)
The Foxman (1990)
Woodsong (1990)
The River (1991)
The Boy Who Owned the School (1991)
The Night the White Deer Died (1991)

Tiltawhirl John (1992)

The Monument (1993)

Harris and Me (1993)

Nightjohn (1993)

Mr. Tucket (1994)

The Car (1994)

Call Me Francis Tucket (1995)

The Rifle (1995)

The Tent (1995)

Brian's Winter (1996)

Father Water, Mother Woods: Essays on Fishing and Hunting in the North Woods (1996)

Tucket's Ride (1997)

The Schernoff Diaries (1997)

My Life in Dog Years (1998)

Soldier's Heart (1998)

The Transall Saga (1998)

My Life in Dog Years (1998)

Tucket's Gold (1999)

The Haymeadow (1999)

Canoe Days (1999)

Alida's Song (1999)

Canyons (1999)

Brian's Return (1999)

Danger on Midnight River (1999)

Popcorn Days and Buttermilk Nights (1999)

Hatchet (1999)

Dogsong (2000)

Tucket's Home (2000)

The White Fox Chronicles: Escape, Return, Breakout (2000)

The Beet Fields: Memories of a Sixteenth Summer (2000)

Caught by the Sea: My Life on Boats (2001)

Dancing Carl (2001)

Puppies, Dogs, and Blue Northers: Reflections on Being Raised by a Pack of Sled Dogs (2002)

How Angel Peterson Got His Name (2003)

Shelf Life: Stories by the Book (2003)

Brian's Hunt (2003)

The Quilt (2004)

The Time Hackers (2005)

Interesting Information:

He ran away from home at 14 to tour with a traveling carnival.

Three of his books are Newbery Honor books.

He loves to interact with his fans.

Web Site: http://www.garypaulsen.com

Contact:

c/o Children's Publicity

1540 Broadway

New York, NY 10036

Author: Rodman Philbrick

Birthplace: Boston, Massachusetts
Date of Birth: 1951
Current Home: Maine and Florida Keys

Titles:

Freak the Mighty (1993)
The Haunting (1995)
The Horror (1995)
The Final Nightmare (1995)
The Fire Pony (1996)
Strange Invaders (1997)
Things (1997)
Brain Stealers (1997)
Abduction (1998)
Max the Mighty (1998)
REM World (2000)
The Last Book in the Universe (2000)

Interesting Information:

He started writing in sixth grade but it was not "cool," so he became a "secret writer."
Once he stopped trying to write literary works and began telling stories, his books sold.
He says he has a kid's voice in his head that tells him what to write.

Web Site: http://www.rodmanphilbrick.com/

Contact:

P.O. Box 4149
Portsmouth, NH 03802-4149

Author: Philip Pullman

Birthplace: Norwich, England
Date of Birth: October 19, 1946
Current Home: Oxford, England

Titles:

Spring-Heeled Jack: A Story of Bravery and Evil (1989)
The Broken Bridge (1990)
The White Mercedes (1992)
The Firework Maker's Daughter (1995)
The Golden Compass (1995)
The Subtle Knife (1997)
Clockwork: Or All Wound Up (1998)
The Amber Spyglass (1999)

Interesting Information:

As a child he loved reading comic books, especially Superman and Batman.
He has been given the highest award given for children's literature in England.
He writes in a shed in the garden behind his home in England.

Web Site: http://www.philip-pullman.com

Contact:

E-mail: feedback@philip-pullman.com

Author: J. K. Rowling

Birthplace: Chipping Sodbury, England

Date of Birth: July 31, 1965

Current Home: Edinburgh, Scotland

Titles:

Harry Potter and the Sorcerer's Stone (1997)

Harry Potter and the Chamber of Secrets (1998)

Harry Potter and the Prisoner of Azkaban (1999)

Harry Potter and the Goblet of Fire (2000)

Harry Potter and the Order of the Phoenix (2003)

Interesting Information:

Before she sold her first book, she was on welfare.

She always wanted to be a writer.

Some of the names in the book are made up and some are real.

Web Site: http://www.jkrowling.com

Contact:

c/o Scholastic, Inc.

555 Broadway

New York, NY 10012

Author: Louis Sachar

Birthplace: East Meadow, New York

Date of Birth: March 20, 1954

Current Home: Austin, Texas

Titles:

Sideways Stories from Wayside School (1978)

There's a Boy in the Girl's Bathroom (1987)

The Boy Who Lost His Face (1989)

Wayside School Is Falling Down (1989)

Sideways Arithmetic from Wayside School (1989)

Dogs Don't Tell Jokes (1991)

More Sideways Arithmetic from Wayside School (1994)

Wayside School Gets a Little Stranger (1995)

Holes (1998)

Stanley Yelnats's Survival Guide to Camp Green Lake (2003)

Interesting Information:

He especially liked math in school but began to love reading in high school.

During college, he worked as a teacher helper and was known as Louis the Yard Teacher, because he always supervised the kids at lunch recess.

He went to law school, passed the bar exam, but decided he wanted to write books.

Web Site: http://www.louissachar.com/

Contact:

c/o Farrar, Straus and Giroux

19 Union Square West

New York, NY 10003

Author: Graham Salisbury

    Birthplace: Philadelphia, Pennsylvania

    Date of Birth: April 11, 1944

    Current Home: Portland, Oregon

Titles:

    Blue Skin of the Sea (1992)

    Under the Blood Red Sun (1994)

    Shark Bait (1998)

    Jungle Dogs (1998)

    Lord of the Deep (2001)

    Island Boyz (2002)

Interesting Information:

    He did not read as a child.

    He flunked English twice in college.

    Now he loves to read and encourages everyone who wants to write to read, read, read.

Web Site: http://www.grahamsalisbury.com

Contact:

    E-mail: graham@grahamsalisbury.com

Author: Jon Scieszka

    Birthplace: Flint, Michigan

    Date of Birth: September 8, 1954

    Current Home: Brooklyn, New York

Titles:

    Knights of the Kitchen Table (1991)

    The Not-So-Jolly Roger (1991)

    The Good, the Bad, and the Goofy (1993)

    2095 (1995)

    Tut, Tut (1996)

    Summer Reading Is Killing Me (1998)

    Your Mother Was a Neanderthal (1999)

    Sam Samurai (2001)

    It's All Greek to Me (2001)

    See You Later, Gladiator (2002)

Interesting Information:

    He was a first- and second-grade teacher and studied writing at Columbia University.

    He likes dark humor, but his audience is hardcore silly kids.

    Someone said he makes the book equivalent of a happy meal!

Web Site: http://www.guysread.com

Contact:

    c/o Children's Marketing

    Penguin USA

    345 Hudson Street

    New York, NY 10014

Author: Darren Shan (Darren O'Shaughnessy)

Birthplace: London, England
Date of Birth: July 2, 1972
Current Home: Limerick, Ireland

Titles:

Cirque du Freak: A Living Nightmare (2001)
Vampire's Assistant (2001)
Tunnels of Blood (2003)
Vampire Mountain (2002)
Trials of Death (2003)
Vampire Prince (2003)
Hunters of the Dusk (2004)
Allies of the Night (2004)

Interesting Information:

His real name is Darren O'Shaughnessy; lives in Limerick, Ireland.
He began writing at age 14 and finished his first novel at 17.
He mostly writes for adults; *Cirque Du Freak* was his first book for children.
He made a seven-figure deal with Warner Bros. for the movie writes to the first two Cirque books.

Web Site: http://www.darrenshan.com

Contact:

c/o Paul Kenny
Rahina
Clarina
County Limerick, Ireland

Author: Neal Shusterman

Birthplace: New York, New York
Date of Birth: November 12, 1962
Current Home: Dove Canyon, California

Titles:

Shadow Club (1988)
Dissidents (1989)
Speeding Bullet (1991)
What Daddy Did (1991)
Kid Heroes (1991)
The Eyes of Kid Midas (1992)
Neal Shusterman's Darkness Creeping: Tales to Trouble Your Sleep (1993)
Neal Shusterman's Darkness Creeping II: More Tales to Trouble Your Sleep (1995)
Scorpian Shards (1995)
Mindstorms: Stories to Blow Your Mind (1996)
The Dark Side of Nowhere (1997)
Mindtwisters: Stories to Shred Your Head (1997)
Downsiders (1999)
Mindbenders: Stories to Warp Your Brain (2000)
Mindquakes: Stories to Shatter Your Brain (2002)
Shadow Club Rising (2002)
Shattered Sky (2003)

The Schwa Was Here (2004)

Interesting Information:

Charlie & the Chocolate Factory and the movie *Jaws* influenced his decision to become a writer.

As a summer camp counselor he became known as the storyteller.

Books played an important part in his life as he was growing up.

Web Site: http://www.storyman.com/

Contact:

PO Box 18516

Irvine, CA 92623-8516

Email: nstoryman@aol.com

Author: William Sleator

Birthplace: Harve de Grace, Maryland

Date of Birth: February 13, 1945

Current Home: Boston, Massachusetts

Titles:

Oddballs (1995)

Others See Us (1995)

Interstellar Pig (1997)

Singularity (1997)

The Beasties (1997)

The Night the Heads Came (1998)

The Boxes (1998)

The Duplicate (1999)

Rewind (1999)

The Boy Who Reversed Himself (2001)

House of Stairs (2001)

Into the Dream (2001)

Marco's Millions (2001)

Parasite Pig (2002)

Interesting Information:

He was a rehearsal pianist for the Boston Ballet Company before he started writing.

He is considered to be the country's most original science fiction writer for teens.

He has a second home in Thailand.

Web Site: http://www.tycho.org./sleator.shtml

Contact:

77 Worcester Street

Boston, MA 02118

c/o Puffin Publicity

375 Hudson Street

New York, NY 10014

E-mail: wsleator@aol.com

Author: Lemony Snicket (Daniel Handler)

Birthplace: San Francisco, California

Date of Birth: 1970

Current Home: Sacramento, California

Titles:

The Bad Beginning (1999)
The Reptile Room (1999)
The Wide Window (2000)
The Miserable Mill (2000)
The Austere Academy (2000)
The Ersatz Elevator (2001)
The Vile Village (2001)
The Hostile Hospital (2001)
The Carnivorous Carnival (2002)
Lemony Snicket: The Unauthorized Autobiography (2002)
The Slippery Slope (2003)
The Grim Grotto (2004)

Interesting Information:

His real name is Daniel Handler.
He attended Lowell High School in San Francisco.
He is married and lives in San Francisco.

Web Site: http://www.lemonysnicket.com

Contact:

c/o HarperCollins
1350 Avenue of the Americas
New York, NY 10019

Author: Jerry Spinelli

Birthplace: Norristown, Pennsylvania
Date of Birth: February 1, 1941
Current Home: Phoenixville, Pennsylvania

Titles:

Who Put that Hair in My Toothbrush? (1984)
Night of the Whale (1985)
Jason and Marceline (1986)
Maniac Magee (1990)
Who Ran My Underwear Up the Flagpole? (1992)
Picklemania (1993)
Do the Funky Pickle (1995)
Fourth Grade Rats (1996)
Crash (1996)
Wringer (1997)
Knots in My Yo-Yo String: The Autobiography of a Kid (1998)
The Library Card (1999)
Stargirl (2000)
Space Station Seventh Grade (2001)
Loser (2002)
The Mighty Crashman (2002)
Milkweed (2003)

Interesting Information:

As a child he wanted to become a major league shortstop.
He first tried to write for adults but was unsuccessful.

He married a woman with six children and started writing for kids.
Web Site: http://www.jerryspinelli.com
Contact:

E-mail: jerry@jerryspinelli.com

Author: Todd Strasser (Morton Rhue)

Birthplace: New York, New York
Date of Birth: May 5, 1950
Current Home: Larchmont, New York

Titles:

The Wave (1981)
Addams Family Values (1993)
Help! I'm Trapped in My Teacher's Body (1994)
Help! I'm Trapped in My Sister's Body (1997)
Help! I'm Trapped in Santa's Body (1997)
How I Created My Perfect Prom Date (1998)
Buzzard's Feast (1999)
Help! I'm Trapped in a Vampire's Body (2000)
Help! I'm Trapped in a Professional Wrestler's Body (2000)
Don't Get Caught Driving the School Bus (2000)
Give a Boy a Gun (2000)
Don't Get Caught in the Girl's Locker Room (2001)
Help! I'm Trapped in a Supermodel's Body (2001)
Con-Fidence (2002)
Thief of Dreams (2003)
Take-Off: Impact Zone (2004)
Close Out: Impact Zone (2004)
Cut Back: Impact Zone (2004)
Can't Get There from Here (2004)

Interesting Information:

He has published more than 100 books, and in three years he wrote/published 24 books.
He is very concerned about school violence and how readily available guns are.
He is currently writing a book on homeless street kids.
Web Site: http://www.toddstrasser.com
Contact:

c/o Scholastic, Inc.
555 Broadway
New York, NY 10012

Author: Theodore Taylor

Birthplace: Statesville, North Carolina
Date of Birth: June 23, 1921
Current Home: Laguna Beach, California

Titles:

Air Raid—Pearl Harbor!: The Story of December 7, 1941 (1971)
The Cay (1987)
Sniper (1989)
The Trouble with Tuck (1989)

The Weirdo (1991)
Tuck Triumphant (1991)
Magnificent Mitscher (1991)
Timothy of the Cay (1993)
Walking Up a Rainbow (1994)
Sweet Friday Island (1994)
The Bomb (1995)
Rogue Wave: And Other Red-Blooded Sea Stories (1996)
A Sailor Returns (2001)
Lord of the Kill (2002)
The Boy Who Could Fly Without a Motor (2002)
The Maldonado Miracle (2003)
Teetoncey (2004)
The Odyssey of Ben O'Neal (2004)
Teetoncey and Ben O'Neal (2004)
Ice Drift (2005)

Interesting Information:

He thinks of himself as a reporter.

He joined the Merchant Marines at age 21.

He writes seven days a week except during football season, when he takes the weekends off.

Web Site: http://www.theodoretaylor.com

Contact:

Publicity Dept.
Bantam Doubleday Dell
1540 Broadway
New York, NY

Author: Jacqueline Woodson

Birthplace: Columbus, Ohio
Date of Birth: February 12, 1963
Current Home: Brooklyn, New York

Titles:

The Dear One (1991)
From the Notebooks of Melanin Sun (1995)
The House You Pass on the Way (1997)
If You Come Softly (1998)
Lena (1998)
Miracle's Boys (2000)
Hush (2002)
Locomotion (2003)
Behind You (2004)

Interesting Information:

In fifth grade she edited her school's literary magazine.

She does not believe in censorship.

She writes about things that actually happen to kids that adults don't want to talk about.

Web Site: http://www.jacquelinewoodson.com

Contact:

    c/o Bantam Doubleday Dell
    1540 Broadway
    New York, NY 10036

Author: Jane Yolen

    Birthplace: New York, New York
    Date of Birth: February 11, 1939
    Current Home: Hatfield, Massachusetts

Titles:

    Dragon's Blood (1982)
    Children Of The Wolf (1984)
    A Sending Of Dragons (1987)
    The Devil's Arithmetic (1988)
    Dragon's Boy (1990)
    Wizard's Hall (1991)
    Hobby (1992)
    Heart's Blood (1994)
    Passager (1996)
    Merlin (1996)
    Armageddon Summer (1998)
    Here There Be Dragons (1998)
    Tartan Magic: The Pictish Child (1999)
    Tartan Magic: The Wizard's Map (1999)
    Queen's Own Fool (2000)
    Young Heroes: Odysseus in the Serpent Maze (2001)
    Tartan Magic: Bagpiper's Ghost (2002)
    Sword of the Rightful King (2003)
    Young Heroes: Jason and the Gorgon's Blood (2004)

Interesting Information:

    Both of Jane's parents and her brothers are writers.
    She has published well over 250 books—she writes for all grade levels and in multiple genres.
    She calls herself and "Arthurholic."

Web Site: http://www.janeyolen.com

Contact:

    E-mail: janeyolen@aol.com

Appendix B

Magazine Information

The following magazines are indexed in a recent volume of *Children's Magazine Guide*. The annotations provide a brief description of each publication's contents and audience. We recommend all the magazines and strongly urge our subscribers to call or write to individual publishers to obtain a sample copy. Note: Subscription prices are per year and in U.S. dollars, including pricing information for Canada (C), Mexico (M), and other foreign countries. Subscription prices are subject to change and may not include applicable taxes, such as Canada's GST.

The Children's Magazine Guide: A Subject Index to Children's Magazines and Web Sites is published at the end of each month by Libraries Unlimited, 88 Post Road West, Westport, CT 06881. See http://www.childrensmag.com for subscription pricing and information. Thank you to Kristina Sheppard, Managing Editor, for allowing us to include the following list of magazines from the *Children's Magazine Guide*:

Ask

Carus Publishing Company
P.O. Box 9304
La Salle, IL 61301
(800) 821-0115
www.askmag.net
The best in science, history, technology, and the arts.
Ages 7-10. 9 issues.
US $32.97; C/Foreign $44.97

Biography Today

Omnigraphics, Inc.
P.O. Box 625
Holmes, PA 19043
(800) 234-1340
www.omnigraphics.com

Profiles 10 contemporary newsmakers per issue from fields such as entertainment, literature, politics, and sports.

Ages 10-15. 3 issues annually.

US and foreign $60.00

AUTHORS Series

Profiles 10 authors per volume.

Ages 10-15. 2 volumes annually.

US and foreign $39.00 per volume.

Biografias Hoy

Biography Today in Spanish.

Ages 10-15. 2 volumes annually.

US and foreign $39.00 per volume.

PERFORMING ARTISTS Series

Profiles 10 performing artists per volume.

Ages 10-15. 2 volumes annually.

US and foreign $39.00 per volume.

SCIENTISTS & INVENTORS Series

Profiles 10 scientist and inventors per volume.

Ages 10-15. 2 volumes annually.

US and foreign $39.00 per volume.

SPORTS Series

Profiles 10-15 athletes per volume.

Ages 10-15. 2 volumes annually.

US and foreign $39.00 per volume.

Boys' Life

Boy Scouts of America

P.O. Box 152079

Irving, TX 75015-2079

(972) 580-2088

www.boyslife.org

Sports, hobbies, outdoor skills, Scouting.

Ages 6-18. Monthly.

US $21.60; C/Foreign $39.60

Boys' Quest

Bluffton News Publishing Company

P.O. Box 227

Bluffton, OH 45817-0227

(800) 358-4732

www.boysquest.com

Fiction and nonfiction written specifically for boys. Science column, math puzzlers. Each issue a different theme.

Ages 6-12. 6 issues.

US $22.95; C/Foreign $28.95

Calliope

Cobblestone Publishing Company
30 Grove Street, Suite C
Peterborough, NH 03458
800/821-0115
www.cobblestonepub.com
World history through the Renaissance period.
Ages 9-15. 9 issues.
US $29.95; C/Foreign $39.95

Career World

Weekly Reader Corporation
3001 Cindel Drive
Delran, NJ 08075
(800) 446-3355
www.weeklyreader.com/store
Career guidance.
Ages 13-18. 6 issues.
US $34.48; Classroom orders $9.95

Children's Digest

Children's Better Health Institute
P.O. Box 420235, 11 Commerce Boulevard
Palm Coast, FL 32142
(386) 447-6302
www.childrensdigestmag.org
Stories, articles and activities on good health habits.
Ages 8-10. 6 issues.
US $22.95; C $34.95; Other foreign $32.95

Cobblestone

Carus Publishing Company
30 Grove Street, Suite C
Peterborough, NH 03458
(800) 821-0115
www.cobblestonepub.com
Themed issues focusing on American history.
Ages 9-14. 9 issues.
US $29.95; C/Foreign $41.95

Cricket

Carus Publishing Company
P.O. Box 9304
La Salle, IL 61301

(800) 821-0115
www.cricketmag.com
Fiction, folklore, nonfiction, and poetry.
Ages 6-12. Monthly.
US $35.97; C/Foreign $47.97

Current Events

Weekly Reader Corporation
3001 Cindel Drive
Delran, NJ 08075
(800) 446-3355
www.weeklyreader.com/store
National and foreign news.
Ages 10-16. 25 issues.
US $34.48; Classroom orders $8.95

Current Health

Weekly Reader Corporation
3001 Cindel Drive
Delran, NJ 08075
(800) 446-3355
www.weeklyreader.com/store
Health and education and advice.
Ages 8-12. 8 issues.
US $34.48; Classroom orders $9.95

Current Science

Weekly Reader Corporation
3001 Cindel Drive
Delran, NJ 08075
(800) 446-3355
www.weeklyreader.com/store
Recent developments in science and health.
Ages 10-16. 16 issues.
US $34.50; Classroom orders $9.75

Dig

Cobblestone Publishing Company
30 Grove Street, Suite C
Peterborough, NH 03458
(800) 821-0115
www.digonsite.com
Themed issues focusing on discoveries and recent developments in archaeology and related subjects.
Ages 9-14. 9 issues.
US $32.97; C/Foreign $44.97

Disney Adventures

Buena Vista Magazines, Inc.
P.O. Box 37287
Boone, IA 50037
(800) 829-5146
http://disney.go.com/DisneyAdventures
Behind the scenes of movies, music, TV, and cartoons.
Ages 6-12. 10 issues.
US $14.97; C/Foreign $24.97

Dolphin Log

The Cousteau Society
710 Settlers Landing Road
Hampton, VA 23669
(800) 441-4395
www.dolphinlog.org
Exploration of oceans, rivers, waterways, and marine life.
Ages 7-13. 6 issues.
US $20.00; C/Foreign $32.00

Faces

Cobblestone Publishing Company
30 Grove Street, Suite C
Peterborough, NH 03458
(800) 821-0115
www.cobblestonepub.com
Theme-oriented issues on geography and world cultures.
Ages 8-14. 9 issues.
US $29.95; C/Foreign $41.95

Footsteps

Cobblestone Publishing Company
30 Grove Street, Suite C
Peterborough, NH 03458
(800) 821-0115
www.footstepsmagazine.com
African-American history.
Ages 9-15. 5 issues.
US $23.95; C/Foreign $35.95

Fun for Kidz

Bluffton News Publishing Company
P.O. Box 227
Bluffton, OH 45817-0227
(800) 358-4732
(419) 358-4610
www.funforkidz.com
Educational and fun activities around a theme for boys and girls.
Ages 6-12. 6 issues.
US $22.95; C/Foreign $28.95

Highlights for Children

P.O. Box 2182
Marion, OH 43306-8282
(888) 876-3809
www.Highlights.com
Stories and articles, puzzles, word games, and craft activities.
Ages 2-12. Monthly.
US $29.64; C $43.72; Other foreign $41.64

Junior Scholastic

Scholastic Inc.
2931 E. McCarty St., P.O. Box 3710
Jefferson City, MO 65102-3710
(800) 724-6527
www.juniorscholastic.com
For price in Canada, write:
Scholastic Canada Ltd.
175 Hillmount Rd.
Markham, ON L6C 1Z7
800/268-3860, www.scholastic.ca.
U.S. and world affairs, current events, history, citizenship, and geography.
Ages 11-15. 18 issues.
US $12.75. Mention Code 3756.

Kids Discover

P.O. Box 54205
Boulder, CO 80328-4205
(800) 284-8276
212/677-4457
www.kidsdiscover.com
Themed issues on various subjects.
Ages 6-12. 12 issues.
US $26.95

Know Your World Extra

Weekly Reader Corporation
3001 Cindel Dr.
Delran, NJ 08075
(800) 446-3355
www.weeklyreader.com/store
High-interest news articles, true-life adventures, and challenging activities.
Ages 11-17. 12 issues.
US $34.50; Classroom orders $10.50

Muse

Carus Publishing Company
P.O. Box 9304
La Salle, IL 61301
(800) 821-0115
www.cricketmag.com
Written and designed to get kids to ask questions and think for themselves. Explores science,
    history, and the arts.
Ages 10 and up. 9 issues.
US $32.97; C/Foreign $44.97

National Geographic Kids

National Geographic Society
P.O. Box 63001
Tampa, FL 33663-3001
(800) 647-5463
www.nationalgeographic.com/ngkids
Wild animals, pets, science, outdoors, hobbies, and sports explored through articles, photographs,
    games, and posters.
Ages 7-13. 10 issues.
US $19.95; C $26.00; Other foreign $29.95

National Wildlife

National Wildlife Federation
11100 Wildlife Center Drive
Reston, VA 20190-5362
(800) 588-1650
www.nwf.org
Photographs and articles on wildlife conservation, research, and ecology.
Ages 12 and up. 6 issues.
US $15.00

Odyssey

Cobblestone Publishing Company
30 Grove Street, Suite C
Peterborough, NH 03458
(800) 821-0115
www.odysseymagazine.com
Physical science, astronomy, and earth and space science.
Ages 10-15. 9 issues.
US $29.95; C/Foreign $41.95

Owl

Bayard Canada
25 Boxwood Lane
Buffalo, NY 14227-2707
In Canada:
P.O. Box 726, Markham Station Main
Markham, ON L3P 7V9
(800) 551-6957
www.owlkids.com
Articles and photographs featuring animals, science, and nature.
Ages 9-13. 10 issues.
US $27.99; C $27.99; Other foreign $47.99

Plays

Sterling Partners, Inc.
P.O. Box 600160
Newton, MA 02460-0002
(800) 630-5755
www.playsmag.com
Original one-act plays and sketches for elementary, middle, and upper grades.
Ages 8-18. 7 issues.
US $33.00; C $41.00; Other foreign $53.00

Ranger Rick

National Wildlife Federation
P.O. Box 2049
Harlin, IA 51593-0269
(800) 611-1599
www.nwf.org
Science, conservation, and nature study via articles, photographs, and activities.
Ages 7-12. Monthly.
US $17.00; C/Foreign $29.00

Read

Weekly Reader Corporation
3001 Cindel Drive
Delran, NJ 08075
(800) 446-3355
www.weeklyreader.com/read
Short stories, plays, book excerpts, word games, and activities to develop reading and writing skills.
Ages 12-16. 18 issues.
US $34.50; Classroom orders $9.95

Scholastic Art

Scholastic Inc.
2931 E. McCarty Street, P.O. Box 3710
Jefferson City, MO 65102-3710
(800) 724-6527
www.scholastic.com
For price in Canada, write:
Scholastic Canada Ltd.
175 Hillmount Road
Markham, ON L6C 1Z7
(800) 268-3860, www.scholastic.ca
Covers art history and studio art.
Ages 12-18. 6 issues.
US $19.95. Mention Code 3756.

Scholastic Choices

Scholastic Inc.
2931 E. McCarty Street, P.O. Box 3710
Jefferson City, MO 65102-3710
(800) 724-6527
www.scholastic.com
For price in Canada, write:
Scholastic Canada Ltd.
175 Hillmount Road
Markham, ON L6C 1Z7
(800) 268-3860, www.scholastic.ca
Family and consumer science, health and nutrition, plus practical real-life skills, and career advice.
Ages 12-18. 6 issues.
US $10.75. Mention Code 3756.

Scholastic Math

Scholastic Inc.
2931 E. McCarty Street, P.O. Box 3710
Jefferson City, MO 65102-3710
(800) 724-6527

www.scholastic.com
For price in Canada write:
Scholastic Canada Ltd.
175 Hillmount Road
Markham, ON L6C 1Z7
(800)268-3860
www.scholastic.ca
Math skills and problem-solving with high-interest teen features and activities.
Ages 11-15. 12 issues.
US $31.95. Mention Code 3756.

Scholastic News

Scholastic Inc.
2931 E. McCarty Street, P.O. Box 3710
Jefferson City, MO 65102-3710
(800) 724-6527
www.scholasticnews.com
For price in Canada, write:
Scholastic Canada Ltd.
175 Hillmount Road
Markham, ON L6C 1Z7
(800) 268-3860, www.scholastic.ca
Current events newsweekly with timely stories and features.
Scholastic News-4, Ages 8-10
Scholastic News-Sr, Ages 10-12
24 issues.
US $4.90. Mention Code 3756.

Scholastic Scope

Scholastic Inc.
2931 E. McCarty Street, P.O. Box 3710
Jefferson City, MO 65102-3710
(800) 724-6527
www.scholastic.com
For price in Canada, write
Scholastic Canada Ltd.
175 Hillmount Road
Markham, ON L6C 1Z7
(800) 268-3860
www.scholastic.ca
Short stories, plays, teen-interest nonfiction articles, vocabulary, and grammar.
Ages 10-14. 18 issues.
US $11.45. Mention Code 3756.

Science World

Scholastic Inc.
2931 E. McCarty Stret, P.O. Box 3710
Jefferson City, MO 65102-3710
(800) 268-3848
www.scholastic.com
For price in Canada, write:
Scholastic Canada Ltd.
175 Hillmount Road
Markham, ON L6C 1Z7
(800) 268-3860, www.scholastic.ca
Recent developments in science and technology, experiments, features, and activities covering all
   areas of science.
Ages 12-16. 13 issues.
US $12.65. Mention Code 3756.

Sports Illustrated for Kids

Time Inc.
P.O. Box 60001
Tampa, FL 33660-0001
(800) 992-0196
www.sikids.com
Coaching tips, sports celebrities, informative articles, and sports stories.
Ages 8-14. Monthly.
US $31.95; C $39.95; Other foreign $49.00

Stone Soup

Children's Art Foundation
P.O. Box 83
Santa Cruz, CA 95063
(800) 447-4569
www.stonesoup.com
Stories, poems, book reviews, and illustrations by young writers and artists.
Ages 8-13. 6 issues.
US $34.00; C/M $40.00; Other Foreign $46.00

Superscience

Scholastic Inc.
2931 E. McCarty Street, P.O. Box 3710
Jefferson City, MO 65102-3710
(800) 724-6527
www.scholastic.com
For price in Canada, write:
Scholastic Canada Ltd.
175 Hillmount Road

Markham, ON L6C 1Z7
(800) 268-3860, www.scholastic.ca
Science discoveries in the news, technology, and hands-on science experiments.
Ages 7-12. 8 issues.
US $29.95 Mention Code 3756.

Teen Newsweek

Weekly Reader Corporation
3001 Cindel Drive
Delran, NJ 08075
(800) 446-3355
www.weeklyreader.com/teens/newsweek
Covers news including politics, sports, and science through cover stories, debates, and worksheets.
Ages 11-14. 26 issues.
US $9.85

Teen People

Time Inc.
P.O. Box 30651
Tampa, FL 33630-0651
(800) 284-0200
www.teenpeople.com
Celebrity profiles, current events, advice, fashion and beauty, and teen-interest stories.
Ages 12-19. 10 issues.
US $15.97; C $21.95

Time for Kids

Time Inc.
P.O. Box 60001
Tampa, FL 33660-0001
TFK-NS: (800) 950-5954
TFK-WR: (800) 777-8600
www.timeforkids.com
Weekly news magazine with high-interest, nonfiction articles and features.
News Scoop Edition, Ages 7-9
World Report Edition, Ages 9-12
26 issues.
US $24.95

Weekly Reader

Weekly Reader Corporation
3001 Cindel Drive
Delran, NJ 08075
(800) 446-3355
www.weeklyreader.com/store

Theme and news-based issues for high-interest nonfiction reading.
Weekly Reader 4, Ages 8-10.
Weekly Reader Sr., Ages 10-12.
25 issues.
US $24.95; Classroom orders $3.75

Yes Mag: Canada's Science Magazine for Kids

Peter Piper Publishing Inc.
3968 Long Gun Place
Victoria, BC V8N 3A9
(250) 477-5543
E-mail: info@yesmag.ca
www.yesmag.ca
Explores the worlds of science, technology, engineering, and mathematics.
Ages 8-14. 6 issues.
US $21.00; C $16.50; Other foreign $25.00

Zoobooks

Wildlife Education, Ltd.
P.O. Box 85384
San Diego, CA 92186-5384
(800) 992-5034
www.zoobooks.com
Each issue features a different animal or group of animals through educational articles, photographs,
    illustrations, posters, and puzzles.
Ages 5-14. Monthly.
US $22.95; C $31.95; Other foreign $33.95

Works Cited

Booth, David. 2002. *Even Hockey Players Read: Boys, Literacy, and Learning*. Pembroke Publishers Limited.

Conlin, Michelle. 2003. "The New Gender Gap: From Kindergarten to Grad School Boys Are Becoming the Second Sex." *Business Week* (May 26): 75–82.

Connell, Diane, and Betsy Gunzelmann. 2004. "The New Gender Gap." *Scholastic Instructor* (March): 14–17.

Galley, Michelle. 2002. "Research: Boys to Men." *Education Week* (January 23): 26–27.

Gurian, Michael. 2001. *Boys and Girls Learn Differently: A Guide for Parents and Teachers*. Jossey-Bass.

Moir, Anne, and David Jessel. 1992. *Brain Sex: The Real Difference between Men and Women*. Delta.

Mulrine, Anna. 2001. "Are Boys the Weaker Sex?" *U.S. News & World Report* (July 20): 41–47.

Newkirk, Thomas. 2002. *Misreading Masculinity: Boys, Literacy, and Popular Culture*. Heinemann.

Pollack, William, and Kathleen Cushman. 2001. *Real Boys Workbook: The Definitive Guide to Understanding and Interacting with Boys of All Ages*. Villard (Random House).

Smith, Michael, and Jeffrey Wilhelm. 2003. *Reading Don't Fix No Chevy's: Literacy in the Lives of Young Men*. Heinemann.

Sullivan, Michael. 2003. *Connecting Boys with Books: What Libraries Can Do*. Chicago: American Library Association.

Wilhelm, Jeff. 2001. "It's a Guy Thing." *Voices from the Middle* (December): 60–63.

Resources

Angelillo, Janet. *Writing about Reading: From Book Talk to Literary Essays, Grades 3–8*. Heinemann, 2003.

Booth, David. *Even Hockey Players Read: Boys, Literacy, and Learning*. Pembroke Publishers Limited, 2002.

Brozo, William. *To Be a Boy, to Be a Reader: Engaging Teen and Preteen Boys in Active Literacy*. International Reading Association, 2002.

Daniels, Harvey. *Literature Circles: Voice and Choice in Book Clubs and Reading Groups*. Stenhouse, 2001.

———. *Literature Circles: Voice and Choice in the Student-Centered Classroom*. Stenhouse, 1994.

Day, Jeni. *Moving Forward with Literature Circles: How to Plan, Manage, and Evaluate Literature Circles That Deepen Understanding and Foster a Love of Reading*. Scholastic Professional Books, 2002.

Drew, Bernard. *100 More Popular Young Adult Authors*. Libraries Unlimited, 2002.

Gillespie, John and Catherine Barr. *Best Books for Middle School and Junior High Readers*. Libraries Unlimited, 2004.

Gurian, Michael. *Boys and Girls Learn Differently: A Guide for Parents and Teachers*. Jossey- Bass, 2001.

———. *The Good Son: Shaping the Moral Development of Our Boys and Young Men*. J.P. Tarcher/Putnam, 1999.

———. *What Stories Does My Son Need? A Guide to Books and Movies that Build Character in Boys*. Putnam, 2000.

———. *The Wonder of Boys: What Parents, Mentors, and Educators Can Do to Shape Boys into Exceptional Men*. J.P. Tarcher/Putnam, 1997.

Herz, S. *From Hinton to Hamlet: Building Bridges between Young Adult Literature and the Classics*. Greenwood Press, 1996.

Hill, Bonnie Campbell, Katherine L. Schlick Noe, and Nancy Johnson. *Literature Circles Resource Guide: Teaching Suggestions, Forms, Sample Book Lists and Database*. Christopher-Gordon Publications, Inc., 2001.

Jobe, Ron, and Mary Dayton-Sakari. *Info-Kids: How to Use Nonfiction to Turn Reluctant Readers into Enthusiastic Learners*. Pembroke Publishers Limited, 2002.

Kindlon, Daniel, and Michael Thompson. *Raising Cain: Protecting the Emotional Life of Boys.* Ballantine, 1999.

Knowles, Elizabeth, and Martha Smith. *Reading Rules! Motivating Teens to Read.* Libraries Unlimited, 2001.

———. *Talk About Books! A Guide for Book Clubs, Literature Circles, and Discussion Groups, Grades 4–8.* Libraries Unlimited, 2003.

Lyga, Allyson. *Graphic Novels in Your Media Center: A Definitive Guide.* Libraries Unlimited, 2004.

McCloud, Scott. *Reinventing Comics: How Imagination and Technology Are Revolutionizing an Art Form.* HarperCollins, 2000.

———. *Understanding Comics: The Invisible Art.* HarperCollins, 1993.

McElmeel, Sharron. *Children's Authors and Illustrators Too Good to Miss.* Libraries Unlimited, 2004.

Moir, Anne, and David Jessel. *Brain Sex: The Real Difference between Men and Women.* Delta, 1992.

Neaman, Mimi, and Mary Strong. *Literature Circles: Cooperative Learning for Grades 3-8.* Teacher Ideas Press, 1992.

Newkirk, Thomas. *Misreading Masculinity: Boys, Literacy, and Popular Culture.* Heinemann, 2002.

Noe, Katherine L. Schlick, and Nancy J. Johnson. *Getting Started with Literature Circles.* Christopher-Gordon Publishers, 1999.

Odean, Kathleen. *Great Books for Boys.* Ballantine, 1998.

Pollack, William, and Kathleen Cushman. *Real Boys: Rescuing Our Sons from the Myths of Boyhood.* Holt, 1998.

———. *Real Boys Workbook: The Definitive Guide to Understanding and Interacting with Boys of All Ages.* Villard (Random House), 2001.

Raphael, T., L. Pardo, K. Highfield, and S. McMahon. *Book Club: A Literature-Based Curriculum.* Small Planet Communications, 1997.

Sullivan, Edward T. *Reaching Reluctant Young Adult Readers: A Handbook for Librarians and Teachers.* Scarecrow Press, 2002.

Sullivan, Michael. *Connecting Boys with Books: What Libraries Can Do.* Chicago: American Library Association, 2003.

Thompson, Michael. *Speaking of Boys: Answers to the Most-Asked Questions about Raising Sons.* Ballantine, 2000.

Tiedt, Iris McCellan. *Teaching with Picture Books in the Middle School.* International Reading Association, 2000.

Author Index

Title Index

About The Authors

ELIZABETH KNOWLES is Director of Staff Development at Pine Crest School in Boca Raton, Florida.

MARTHA SMITH is Library Media Specialist at Pine Crest School.